2ND EDITION
ASSESSMENT PACK

Pearson Education Limited
KAO Two
KAO Park
Harlow
Essex CM17 9NA
England
and Associated Companies throughout the world.

www.pearsonELT.com/bigenglish2

© Pearson Education Limited 2017

The right of Mario Herrera and Christopher Sol Cruz to be identified as author of this Work has been asserted by them in accordance with the Copyright, Designs and Patents Act 1988.

All rights reserved; no part of this publication may be reproduced, stored in a retrieval system, or transmitted in any form or by any means, electronic, mechanical, photocopying, recording, or otherwise without the prior written permission of the Publishers

Photocopying: The Publisher grants permission for the photocopying of those pages marked 'photocopiable' according to the following conditions. Individual purchasers may make copies for their own use or for use by the classes they teach. Institutional purchasers may make copies for use by their staff and students, but this permission does not extend to additional institutions or branches. Under no circumstances may any part of this book be photocopied for resale.

First published 2017
Second impression 2019

ISBN: 978-1-2922-3323-9

Set in Heinemann Roman 16/24pt
Printed in Slovakia by Neografia

Acknowledgements

The publisher would like to thank the following for their kind permission to reproduce their photographs:

(Key: b-bottom; c-centre; l-left; r-right; t-top)

123RF.com: 8/1b, 31r, 70/2b, aarrows 56/1c, 56/3b, 57 (cheese), 74/3b, 80r/3, Jacek Chabraszewski 57 (burgers), chrupka 17c, donatas1205 20 (3c), gbh007 17l, highwaystarz 10/2b, 26/2c, kozzi 59/4, Geo Martinez 56/3a, 56/4c, olesiabilkei 26/1b, peterm 10/2c, romrodinka 15/b, 28/3, tnnl03eda 38cr, wavebreakmediamicro 8/1a, 10/3c, 11/a, 26/1a, 40l/3, yarruta 70/4a; **Alamy Stock Photo:** Blend Images 38bc, 39cr, Phovoir 38br, 40r/2, TomBham 82/4, VStock 80tc (left); **Fotolia.com:** Ilike 26/3a, pololia 83/3, Viktor 57 (chips), WavebreakmediaMicro 80tr; **Getty Images:** Diane Collins and Jordan Hollender 8/2b; **Pearson Education Ltd:** Studio 8 8 (b), 8/2c, 10/1b, 16cl, 83/2, Gareth Boden 28/5, Trevor Clifford 42bc/1, Lord and Leverett 12cl, Silverpin Design Company Ltd 11/b, 28/1, Alice McBroom 10/1a, Jules Selmes 8/1c, 10/3a, 12tl, 26/2a, 26/2b, 26/3b, 38bl, Tudor Photography 16cr, Ian Wedgewood 38tl, 42tc/2; **Shutterstock.com:** 321598 39/4, Alan Poulson Photography 53l, alisalipa 74/1a, Andy-pix 39/3, Stephane Angue 62/2, 63bl, 66tr, 76/2b, 76/4c, Artazum 31cr, ayakovlevcom 53r, Volodymyr Burdiak 62/1, 64tr, 66tl, 76/1a, 76/3b, Sergiy Bykhunenko 15/c, 28/2, 83/4, Carlo Dapino 10/2a, 80tc (right), Zhu Difeng 23t, EcoPrint 64bc, 66b, Elnur 39/1, Eviled 31l, fotoban eos 56/1b, 57 (bananas), 74/3c, 80r/1, Fotokostic 39/2, 41/c, 83/1, Douglas Freer 82/3, Goncharuk 56/1a, 57 (carrots), 59/2, 74/2c, 74/4a, 80l/3, Nanette Grebe 38tc, 39br, 41/a, 82/2, Simon Greig 15/d, 64tl, 76/1b, 76/3a, Darrin Henry 8/2a, Horiyan 74/1c, Hurst Photo 10/3b, 10b, 70/1a, Igor Sokolov (breeze) 11/c, Terekhov Igor 20 (2c), JaySi 69bl, 79r, Kamira 12cr, 80tl, Khamidulin Sergey 69bc, 70/2a, 79l, Kitch Bain 59/1, Vladimir Koletic 42bl/2, Rick Lord 53cl, lynnette 20 (1b), Viktar Malyshchyts 57 (pineapple), 58/1, 74/2a, Monkey Business Images 12tr, Morphart Creation 20 (2a, 3a), MrGarry 20 (1c), Amy Myers 15/a, 16bl, Nate A 70/3b, 70/4b, Nattika 57 (potatoes), 58/6, 74/4c, Naypong 62/5, 63bc, William Perugini 40r/3, Pressmaster 69br, Alexander Raths 38tr, 38cl, 39bl, 40l/1, 40r/1, 41/d, 42tl/2, Refat 8 (d), Ian Rentoul 62/4, 66cr, 76/2c, 76/4a, rickyd 63tl, 64bl, 76/1c, 82/1, Rido 10/1c, 26/1c, 26/3c, Eduardo Rivero 62/6, 63br, 64br, 76/3c, Rohit Seth 42bl/1, Julian Rovagnati 16br, sagir 20 (3b), Sergios 42tc/1, Victor Shova 63tc, 64tc, Slava_Kovtun 56/3c, 56/4b, 59/3, 74/2b, 80l/4, Smit 44, 46, 47, 48, 54, 55, Igor Sokolov 8 (a), Bryan Solomon 57 (cookies), spotmatik 28/4, 70/1b, Gary Stone 62/3, 66cl, Pal Teravagimov 63tr, 76/2a, 76/4b, the.grey.squirrel 56/4a, 58/5, 80r/4, Jeff Thrower 17r, topseller 80l/1, travellight 56/2a, 58/3, 74/1b, 80l/2, Diane Uhley 3lcl, Kiselev Andrey Valerevich 38c, 39cl, 40l/2, 41/b, 42tr/2, Veja 8 (c), Dani Vincek 56/2b, 57 (chicken), 58/4, 74/3a, 80r/2, Valentyn Volkov 57 (mango), wavebreakmedia 42br/2, 53cr, Tracy Whiteside 42tl/1, William Milner 20 (1a, 2b), Yellowj 56/2c, 57 (tomatoes), 58/2, 74/4b, Terrie L. Zeller 70/3a

All other images © Pearson Education

Every effort has been made to trace the copyright holders and we apologise in advance for any unintentional omissions. We would be pleased to insert the appropriate acknowledgement in any subsequent edition of this publication.

Illustrated by: Robin Boyer, Tamara Joubert, Jim Peacock, Q2A Media Services, Jose Rubio, Christos Skaltsas, Julia Wolf

Level 2 | Contents

Big English Assessment Pack		iv
Assessment of Young Learners		vi
Test-taking Strategies		x
Scoring in Big English		xii
Student Self-Tracking Progress Charts		xvii
Level 2	Diagnostic Pre-Test	02
Speaking Assessment Prompts		06
Unit 1	Practice Test	08
Unit 1	Unit Test	10
Unit 1	Speaking Assessment Prompts	12
Unit 2	Practice Test	14
Unit 2	Unit Test	16
Unit 2	Speaking Assessment Prompts	18
Unit 3	Practice Test	20
Unit 3	Unit Test	22
Unit 3	Speaking Assessment Prompts	24
Units 1–3	Mastery Test	26
Unit 4	Practice Test	32
Unit 4	Unit Test	34
Unit 4	Speaking Assessment Prompts	36
Unit 5	Practice Test	38
Unit 5	Unit Test	40
Unit 5	Speaking Assessment Prompts	42
Unit 6	Practice Test	44
Unit 6	Unit Test	46
Unit 6	Speaking Assessment Prompts	48
Units 4–6	Mastery Test	50
Unit 7	Practice Test	56
Unit 7	Unit Test	58
Unit 7	Speaking Assessment Prompts	60
Unit 8	Practice Test	62
Unit 8	Unit Test	64
Unit 8	Speaking Assessment Prompts	66
Unit 9	Practice Test	68
Unit 9	Unit Test	70
Unit 9	Speaking Assessment Prompts	72
Units 7–9	Mastery Test	74
Level 2	Final Exam	80
Speaking Assessment Prompts		85
Answer Key and Audioscript		87

Level 2

Big English Assessment Pack

The *Big English Assessment Pack* is a useful evaluation tool with a wealth of activity types assessing the students' language skills. The program balances these assessments throughout each learning year and within individual units.

In this pack, teachers can find five types of tests which will help them form an accurate evaluation of their students' understanding and achievement.

Pre-Tests
Diagnostic Pre-Tests are designed to help place students into a specific level of study that is neither too easy nor too difficult. *Big English* provides six written Diagnostic Pre-Tests (for levels 1 to 6) that evaluate students' current language facility in English. Be sure to administer Pre-Tests in a relaxed and supportive atmosphere, emphasizing that the results will help match students with a level that is both fun and challenging.

Practice Tests
Each level includes nine Practice Tests which provide students with opportunities for review of learned content and rehearsal of test-taking strategies. To use these tests as formative assessments, consider giving students feedback on strengths and weaknesses, rather than scores. Encourage students to ask questions and find information about concepts they do not fully understand and adapt teaching strategies to help students meet their learning goals. In this way, Practice Tests become part of the instructional process as well as preparation for Unit Tests. (Practice Tests can also be used as make-up tests for students absent on test days.)

Unit Tests
Each level also includes nine Unit Tests which correspond to the content material in each of the units and reflect their teaching objectives. These summative tests provide a useful snapshot of student achievement at the end of a unit. They are meant to be graded and included as part of each student's overall assessment.

Mastery Tests
Each Mastery Test assesses student understanding and retention of concepts taught in the previous three units (Units 1–3, Units 4–6, and Units 7–9). These tests help students remember and integrate material learned over time, and assist teachers in decisions regarding which elements of a course need additional review and practice. Like Unit Tests, these are also meant to be graded and included in each student's overall assessment.

Final Exam
The Final Exam for each level assesses student comprehension of the level's key learning objectives.

Level 2

What's new

For this new edition, the tests have been updated to match the new Student's Book content. Additional tests have also been added to provide a more balanced assessment of the four skills. There are brand-new listening and reading tasks as well as a new speaking assessment section with prompts and detailed Teacher notes. In addition, existing content has been modified to provide more variety in the type of tasks, many of which follow the CYLET's specifications. This will provide students with more useful exam preparation.

New speaking and writing checklists and assessment criteria have been introduced which map to the Global Scale of English (GSE) and which will make it easier to assess each student's performance.

Global Scale of English

The Global Scale of English (GSE) is a standardized, granular scale which measures English language proficiency. Unlike some other frameworks which describe attainment in broad bands, the GSE identifies what a learner can do at each point on the scale across speaking, listening, reading, and writing skills. The scale is designed to motivate learners by giving more granular insight into learning progress. Teachers can use the GSE to match a student to the right course materials for their exact level and learning goals.

The badging on the back of your coursebook shows the range of objectives that are covered within the content. Knowing this range helps you select materials with the right level of support and challenge for your students to help them progress. It does not mean that students need to have mastered all objectives below the range before starting the course, or that they will all be 'at' the top of the range by the end.

For more information about how using the GSE can support your planning and teaching, your assessment of your learners, and in selecting or creating additional materials to supplement your core program please go to www.english.com/gse.

Level 2

Assessment of Young Learners

Around the world, students are being introduced to second, or foreign, languages sooner than ever before. The need to measure student achievement is by no means new. However, assessing language learners between the ages of five and twelve requires teachers to be aware of special considerations such as students' social, emotional, and cognitive development; cultural background; and familiarity with different types of texts particularly for those students who wish to complete external standardized tests. Effective assessment also takes into account the school and classroom setting, class materials and activities, and the expectations of both teachers and students.

In *Big English*, students learn language structure and vocabulary in high-interest, thematic contexts using the four communication skills: listening, speaking, reading, and writing. The ratio of these elements varies according to the level, age, and cognitive abilities of the learners.

For the newest and/or youngest learners, a heavier emphasis is placed on listening and speaking; reading and writing tasks are gradually introduced as they become appropriate to students' age and development. For older, more advanced learners, reading and writing instruction plays a more prominent role. Nonetheless, speaking and listening are practiced throughout the program, as students need to develop strong oral communication skills in order to achieve fluency. In *Big English*, students engage in a variety of contextualized activities, each of which focuses on a particular learning objective. These objectives are fully supported by the *Big English Assessment Pack*.

The *Big English* tests provide a wide range of tasks using formats of controlled practice such as multiple choice, true/false, fill in the blank, matching, and labeling. However, fair and accurate assessment in a language classroom reflects not only what students can recognize and produce on a test, but also what they can perform or do as they actually use the language in real or realistic contexts. To evaluate learners' progress fairly and fully, both of these aspects must be part of an effective approach to assessment. Therefore, in *Big English* students are also offered opportunities to express themselves more freely with more open writing tasks and through the speaking assessment.

Level 2

Summative Assessment

A balanced assessment program includes both formative and summative assessment. Considering the role that each of these types of assessment plays in the classroom can help teachers ensure that they are using tools that will accurately measure all aspects of student achievement.

Formative assessment takes place during the instructional process—while students are *forming* their understanding of new concepts. When applying formative assessment strategies, both educators and learners gather evidence and information that is used for the purpose of improving learning. These strategies can provide answers to educators to the following questions:

- Who is or is not understanding the lesson?
- What are the students' strengths and needs?
- What misconceptions do I need to clarify?
- What type of feedback should I give?
- What adjustments should I make to instruction?
- How should students be grouped?
- What differentiation do I need to prepare?

Formative assessment should include a variety of activities, including classroom discussions, peer or group work, homework, as well as traditional tests and quizzes. The important thing to remember about formative assessment is that the method of assessment is not what makes it useful, but the way in which the results are used. Formative assessment is most successful when results are analyzed to determine the current state of student understanding. Results are folded into the classroom experience as teachers take specific actions to improve any deficiencies or correct misunderstandings.

It is obvious that students who take an active role in their own learning have a greater chance for success. Involving students in the assessment process will improve student achievement and motivation (Sadler 1989). The educator can serve as coach or facilitator in this process. Students need to understand learning and performance objectives, identify their current level of comprehension, develop strategies to reach the learning objectives, and address any deficiencies.

Summative assessment gives feedback about what students know and do not know at a particular point in time. These assessments provide evidence of student achievement for the purpose of judging student competence or program effectiveness. Summative assessments usually rank understanding by assigning a letter or number grade. The data gained from summative assessments are generally used to determine how many students are and are not meeting pre-set standards for a program.

Summative assessment is an essential tool for gauging student achievement and verifying instruction, but it cannot stand alone. Because it generally occurs after the learning process, it does not help teachers make instructional adjustments that will improve student progress.

Level 2

Assessment for Learning

Big English has been developed to allow teachers and students multiple opportunities to integrate Assessment for Learning into every lesson. Notes in the *Big English Teacher's Edition* for each level clearly signpost stages in the Assessment for Learning (AfL) process. Assessment opportunities become a natural and integral part of the learning process, leading directly to changes in teaching strategies to ensure students acquire target skills.

A balanced approach to assessment includes frequent informal prompts, games, and other activities that allow students to understand where they are and identify gaps in their understanding. When informal assessments are integrated into the classroom, students take an active role in their own education and seek out the help they need to meet their goals.

One aspect of assessment that is frequently overlooked by traditional approaches is positive reinforcement. All students need to be encouraged by identifying skills they have successfully acquired. Focusing attention only on mistakes or unlearned material creates disengaged, dispirited students. Always be sure to praise students for skills they have successfully acquired before identifying those which need work. Beginning learners are especially responsive to positive feedback.

Self- and Peer-assessment

Involving students in the assessment process helps create a learning community in which all members are working together toward a shared goal. Assessment for Learning asks students to assess their progress frequently, both individually and in groups.

- **Self-assessment** involves students in evaluating their own performance and progress. Self-assessment activities should be planned according to students' age, development level, and cognitive abilities. Very young children can color or draw a happy face, neutral face, or sad face to indicate their feelings about their work; older students can circle words or write descriptive sentences on a chart.

- **Peer-assessment** offers students a collaborative opportunity to share and evaluate their progress with classmates. In peer-assessments, students are trained to give constructive feedback on other students' class work, homework assignments, or tests. Generally, students first give a positive comment or two, followed by questions about something they found confusing or incorrect. Partners or groups can then work together to find solutions. Provide students with models of both strong and weak work to help prepare them to evaluate the work of others.

Level 2

Managing Expectations

Assessment for Learning creates a collaborative environment in which teachers and students work together. Both partners need to be aware of their expectations, and understand when they are reasonable and when they need to be adjusted.

- **Teacher expectations** play a crucial role in preparing students for assessments. Teachers should have high, but reasonable, expectations for student performance. Students who sense a teacher doesn't have high expectations for them or confidence in their ability to learn often lose interest and motivation. There is no long-term sense of satisfaction in dealing with tasks that are not challenging.

In contrast, students who believe a teacher's expectations are too demanding and unrealistic soon begin to give up the struggle. Testing becomes a scary and anxiety-filled experience that reduces confidence and motivation. In setting and communicating expectations for students, it is important to consider the age of the learners, their level of cognitive development, and the number of contact hours they have each week.

- **Student expectations** can affect their assessment experiences. Students can expect a testing atmosphere that is quiet and supportive. They should not be afraid to ask for clarification if they do not understand instructions. Finally, they can expect prompt feedback so that they can evaluate their progress, take pride in achievements, and identify areas that need further attention.

Successful Formal Assessment

It is important to prepare students for any formal assessment. The added transparency of a classroom that follows Assessment for Learning strategies means that students understand why they are being tested and what those results will (and will not) say about their progress.

Test Review and Warm-Up

The day before a test, lead students in a review of unit content presented as a game or team contest that will provide practice for the coming test without causing anxiety. The day of the test, take time to lead students in a warm-up activity that will allow them to switch from thinking in their native language to thinking in English. Having students perform a favorite song or chant from the unit can help them to relax.

Test Information

Students should be told the content and skills the test will cover, how long the test will be, and how the test will be scored. For very young students, it is helpful to provide examples of the test item formats beforehand, such as drawing a circle around a word choice, matching, true/false, and choosing a word from a list to fill in a blank. Students should never be tested using formats they have not worked with before, nor should they have to read test instructions in language they have not seen. Keep formats and instructions simple and similar to those found in the Student's Book.

Copyright © by Pearson Education, Ltd.

Level 2

Test-taking Strategies

Students should be familiar with test-taking strategies that will help them feel confident during formal assessments. Remind students to review their Student's Book, Workbook, corrected homework assignments, and previous tests. In addition, point out the need to get enough sleep the night before and eat a good breakfast the day of the test. A few days before a test, share the following strategies with students to help them prepare.

✓ The best way to do well on tests is to do well in class, from day one.
   - Pay attention every day.
   - Be prepared.
   - Ask questions when you are confused or need help.

✓ Find out about the test you will have from your teacher. This helps you know what to study and what to expect.
   - What material will the test cover?
   - What formats will be on the test?

Check the answer	Multiple-choice	Circle the answer	Interview
Draw	Read and answer	Fill-in-the-blank	True/False
Match	Write		

   - How much time will you have for the test?

✓ Prepare for the test the day before.
   - Choose a comfortable, quiet place to study.
   - Choose a time to study when you aren't tired or sleepy.
   - Review your Student's Book and Workbook.
   - Review your class notebook, worksheets, quizzes, and tests.

✓ Really study.
   - Identify the information you know well and spend a little time reviewing it.
   - Identify the information you don't know well and spend the most time studying it.
   - Read difficult parts aloud or write them down. This helps you concentrate and remember information better.

✓ Try these strategies to help you remember information.
   - Make flash cards or note cards and review them often.
   - Make a drawing or a poster and hang it on a wall you see every day.
   - Use graphic organizers, such as idea maps or outlines, to make sense of material. Organized information is easier to remember.
   - Use songs and chants to remember vocabulary and grammar.

Level 2

- Visualize a picture that illustrates words or ideas you need to remember.

Two meanings of *trunk*:

1. the long, tube-like part of an elephant's face used for feeding and drinking
2. a large, strong box with a lock and key; used for storing objects and for traveling

✓ Use these strategies while you are taking a test. They will help you organize your thoughts and make good use of your time.
  - Have ready two sharp pencils and a good eraser.
  - Write your name on your test as soon as you get it.
  - Listen carefully to your teacher's instructions. Ask questions if you don't understand.
  - Before you begin, look on both sides of your paper. Are there questions you must answer on the other side?
  - Now quickly read all the questions on the test. This will help you decide how to plan your time. (You will need more time for the difficult questions.)
  - Here is one good system for choosing the order of questions to answer.
  1. Begin with a question or two you know the answer to. This helps you relax and feel more confident.
  2. Before the first half of your time is up, go to the difficult questions. Are some questions worth a lot of points? Work on them now, while you still have time.
  3. Leave some easy questions for last, when there isn't much time left. Make sure they are questions you can answer quickly, if necessary.
  4. If there is time, go back to make sure you answered all the questions. Check your answers for possible mistakes.

✓ When your teacher gives your graded test back, look carefully at your wrong answers. This will help you be better prepared for the future.
  - Look at each mistake. Try to figure out the correct answer yourself.
  - If you don't understand why your answer is wrong, ask your teacher.
  - Write each correct answer on your test paper. Keep your test to review together with other materials before your next test.

Level 2

Scoring in Big English

The Diagnostic Pre-Test, Practice and Unit Tests, Mastery Tests, and Final Exam include a score box for teachers to complete. You should allocate a point for every item or question and if a task contains two tasks (e.g. Listen and match. Then write.), then award two points. The use of the scoring system however is up to your discretion and you might prefer to mark the tests using the scores and share the results with your students giving them more explanations and guidance. On the other hand, you could choose to keep the scores secret and provide individual feedback on each student's strength and weaknesses either orally or in writing.

Assessing Speaking

It is important to assess students' speaking skills in settings that are relaxed and tension-free. The *Big English Assessment Pack* offers a variety of speaking activities in every test. Visual prompts are provided and there are detailed teaching notes suggesting questions that the students can be asked. There are also *Challenges* which offer extension ideas for fast finishers or stronger students.

To more accurately evaluate students' performance, it is better for students to perform the speaking test individually or in pairs as an interview. If your teaching settings require it, you can also choose to set up whole-class activities and circulate around the room to listen to the students as they work through the activities. This will allow you to make notes on individual students without making it obvious that you are listening to them, thus reducing the pressure on them. Pause, standing to the side of the student or pairs of students you are evaluating. You may even want to turn your back on the student you are actually listening to, so that the student remains involved with the task and does not focus attention on you or stop because you are listening. In one-on-one interviews, students are of course aware that they are being assessed. You may want to interview just a few students each day over a period of days, or you may want to interview all of your students on one day, while other students are doing work for extra credit, reading, or completing homework assignments.

Checklist with Assessment Criteria

On the next page, you can find a detailed checklist to track students' speaking performance at a glance. It is essentially a set of descriptions of criteria used for assessment in this level. These descriptors are informed by the GSE and CEFR. There is also a rating appropriate for each description, presented in chart form. Descriptors are clearer than simple letter or number grades, and serve as feedback for students (and their parents). Using the rating scale for each descriptor, you can keep track of each student's progress in speaking production, fluency, interaction, and range. Depending on the task you are evaluating, you may not need to fill in every category; check the appropriate boxes, fill in needed information, and make notes that will help you with the evaluation.

Level 2

Speaking Assessment Checklist

Student's name: _____   Class: _____   Test: _____   Date: _____

G = very good   S = satisfactory   U = unsatisfactory

Spoken production and fluency			
1. Can use single words and very short phrases in a formulaic, memorized fashion.	G	S	U
2. Can support meaning without using non-verbal communication.	G	S	U
3. Can use simple phrases with a little hesitation.	G	S	U
Spoken interaction			
4. Can contribute to short exchanges on familiar topics.	G	S	U
5. Can use simple fixed expressions to observe social conventions.	G	S	U
Range			
6. Can use the unit's grammar correctly with support.	G	S	U
7. Can use basic phrases to talk about the unit's topic.	G	S	U
8. Can express simple personal opinions.	G	S	U
Accuracy			
9. Can pronounce target words and phrases though support may be necessary.	G	S	U
10. Can produce intelligible language though errors may be frequent.	G	S	U

Notes: _____

_____

_____

_____

_____

_____

_____

Copyright © by Pearson Education, Ltd.

Level 2

GSE Speaking Descriptors

Global Scale of English: Speaking Assessment Descriptors

	GSE 10–21/<A1	GSE 22–29/A1	GSE 30–35/A2
SPOKEN PRODUCTION AND FLUENCY • Productive ability • Extent of contribution • Pausing and hesitation	Uses single words and very short phrases in a formulaic, memorized fashion (e.g. numbers, colors, *My name is …, My favorite … is…*). Is likely to use non-verbal communication to support meaning. Likely to hesitate and need considerable thinking time.	Uses simple phrases and fixed expressions in a formulaic fashion (e.g. *What's the time?, Can I have a pencil?*). May use non-verbal communication to support meaning. Uses fixed expressions in classroom tasks and activities. Hesitation is likely, although not inevitable.	Uses simple sentences in a less controlled context, with developing confidence (e.g. *My best friend's name is … He has short brown hair. He likes going to the movie theater.*). Can describe in simple terms, moving beyond the formulaic. Can sustain speech beyond short isolated phrases. Hesitation is still possible, but is beginning to attempt recovery/reformulation.
SPOKEN INTERACTION • Ability to understand, contribute to, and maintain interaction • Appropriacy of language and functions • Coherence • Support	Contributes to basic exchanges using single words and/or very simple memorized expressions with support/scaffolding from the other interlocutor (e.g. repetition and/or re-phrasing, modifying speed, supplying missing language, giving non-verbal support, etc.). Uses basic words to observe social conventions (e.g. polite greetings/please/thank you).	Contributes to short exchanges on familiar topic areas with some support, both asking and answering formulaic questions. Uses simple fixed expressions to observe social conventions (e.g. *How are you? Be careful! I'm sorry!*).	Contributes to simple exchanges on topics of personal importance or everyday relevance using simple language and some fixed expressions. May achieve the interactive process (e.g. turn taking) without support. Uses simple fixed expressions to observe social conventions in a widening range of contexts (e.g. introducing people, responding to apologies, politely refusing a request).
RANGE • Grammar and vocab • Topics and contexts	Uses single words and short fixed expressions related to information of personal relevance or the immediate personal environment and situation (e.g. *Hello/Goodbye, Please/Thank you, Sorry?*).	Uses basic phrases/fixed expressions related to family, friends, home life, and personal experiences as well as the immediate classroom environment (e.g. *How do you spell that?, Nice to meet you!*) Can express simple personal opinions (likes/dislikes).	Uses simple, often repetitive language related to own world situations and experiences (e.g. *Let's go to the movie theater, I'd like a hamburger and fries please.*). Has a growing command of the language needed within the classroom to express needs and wants and to complete classroom activities. Contexts are still 'own world centered' but may be broader in range (e.g. their own childhood/their future plans/their friend's routines etc).
ACCURACY • Pronunciation, stress, and intonation • Control of structure, vocabulary, and function	Can produce intelligible language with support and/or modeling from other interlocutors.	Can produce intelligible language with less immediate input, although errors may often still be necessary. Beginning to develop control, although errors frequent and support still needed to achieve communication.	The majority of words are intelligible. Errors may still be evident but there is less need for support to achieve communication.

Level 2

Assessing the Writing

With the writing tasks, you can assess your students' handwriting and their knowledge of spelling of individual words. As the challenge increases across units and levels, you can also assess their ability to express themselves with longer sentences, to structure paragraphs and longer texts.

As a suggested marking scheme, award two points per category: written production, range, and accuracy. So each writing task adds up to six points.

Writing Assessment Checklist

Student's name: _____ Class: _____ Test: _____ Date: _____

G = very good   S = satisfactory   U = unsatisfactory

Written production			
1. Can write the letters of the alphabet correctly (lower and upper case).	G	S	U
2. Can copy words and short phrases correctly.	G	S	U
3. Can write basic sentences with support.	G	S	U
4. Can write short, simple texts with support.	G	S	U
5. Can link simple sentences with 'and' and 'but.'	G	S	U
6. Can produce different text types, e.g. shopping lists, greeting in a card, personal information.	G	S	U
Range			
7. Can use the unit's vocabulary correctly with support.	G	S	U
8. Can use basic structures with support.	G	S	U
Accuracy			
9. Can use capital letters correctly (for names, to start a sentence).	G	S	U
10. Can use the correct spelling of familiar words.	G	S	U
11. Can use a limited range of punctuation.	G	S	U

Notes: _____
_____
_____
_____
_____
_____

Copyright © by Pearson Education, Ltd.

Level 2

GSE Writing Descriptors

Global Scale of English: Writing Assessment Descriptors

	GSE 10–21/<A1	GSE 22–29/A1	GSE 30–35/A2
WRITTEN PRODUCTION • Content and organization • Appropriacy • Coherence and cohesion • Text types • Ability to correct	Can write the letters of the alphabet in upper and lower case. Can copy short words and may be able to copy very short phrases (e.g. *This is Mary.*) once familiarized with them.	Can write basic isolated sentences (e.g. *I can swim. I like dogs and cats.*) with a model. Is able to write short answers to questions in a reading text (e.g. *What color is the book? → It is red.*). May be able to produce short, simple texts (two or three sentences) on a familiar topic, when modeled. Can link simple sentences with basic connectors (e.g. *and* and *but*). Is able to produce a limited number of text types appropriately: can write lists of words (e.g. a shopping list or a categorizing activity for classroom purposes), can complete simple tables/grids or forms with basic personal information and can write an appropriate greeting in a card. Has an awareness of errors (e.g. in spelling) when guided.	Can write simple sentences (e.g. *My friend has brown hair. I don't like doing my homework.*) with a model. May be able to produce simple texts with relevant content (four to six sentences) on a familiar topic, when modeled. Can use simple connecting devices (e.g. *or* or *because*) to link sentences. Is able to produce a small range of text types appropriately, including simple notes and invitations, short, basic descriptions, and lists for specific purposes (e.g. recording an activity). Is able to make corrections to spelling when guided.
RANGE • Topics and contexts • Grammar and vocabulary • Functions	Topics are very familiar and/or related to the immediate environment (e.g. names, numbers, family members, classroom objects, toys, pets, etc.). Grammar and vocabulary are limited to single words and very simple formulaic structures (e.g. *This is …, I am …*).	Topics remain own world centered but may include familiar things seen in pictures/stories (e.g. everyday items, daily activities, etc.). Can produce basic structures and simple vocabulary of personal relevance, with support (e.g. *I like hamburgers.*). Can use language to perform basic functions (e.g. simple personal opinions (likes/dislikes)).	Topics relate to own world situations, knowledge, and experiences (family and friends, their town, simple narratives, etc.). Can produce simple structures with independence (e.g. *Would you like a drink? I went to the park. I usually walk to school, etc.*). Can use vocabulary related to topics. Is able to use fixed phrases to produce some simple functions (e.g. making an invitation or thanking someone) if given a model.
ACCURACY • Spelling and punctuation • Control of structure and vocabulary	Can use capital letters on names and may use a capital to begin a sentence. Can spell simple words correctly when copying from a model. Errors are frequent if not copying from a model, and very common in learners with non-Latin L1 alphabets.	Can punctuate a sentence correctly (using capital letters and periods) and has an awareness of question marks. Can use apostrophes for contractions. Familiar words may be spelled correctly. Has an awareness of very simple spelling rules (e.g. *cat → cats, bus → buses*). May show good control of structure and vocabulary when closely guided by a model. Errors in spelling/orthography are frequent in learners with non-Latin L1 alphabets.	Can accurately use a range of punctuation including commas and possessive apostrophes. Has an awareness of simple spelling rules (e.g. *dance → dancing*). Familiar words are usually spelled correctly; errors may occur with newer lexis. Can control structure and vocabulary when using familiar language: errors are likely with less familiar language in less controlled contexts. Learners with non-Latin L1 alphabets may often make mistakes in spelling/orthography.

Level 2

Student Self-Tracking Progress Charts

Students can keep track of their progress by referring to the *I can* statements at the end of each unit in their Student's Book. They can also use the following chart and fill it in when they receive the results for each test.

My Progress					
	Unit 1	Unit 2	Unit 3	Unit 4	Unit 5
Test score					
Reading	☺ 😐 ☹	☺ 😐 ☹	☺ 😐 ☹	☺ 😐 ☹	☺ 😐 ☹
Listening	☺ 😐 ☹	☺ 😐 ☹	☺ 😐 ☹	☺ 😐 ☹	☺ 😐 ☹
Writing	☺ 😐 ☹	☺ 😐 ☹	☺ 😐 ☹	☺ 😐 ☹	☺ 😐 ☹
Speaking	☺ 😐 ☹	☺ 😐 ☹	☺ 😐 ☹	☺ 😐 ☹	☺ 😐 ☹
My teacher says					

My Progress				
	Unit 6	Unit 7	Unit 8	Unit 9
Test score				
Reading	☺ 😐 ☹	☺ 😐 ☹	☺ 😐 ☹	☺ 😐 ☹
Listening	☺ 😐 ☹	☺ 😐 ☹	☺ 😐 ☹	☺ 😐 ☹
Writing	☺ 😐 ☹	☺ 😐 ☹	☺ 😐 ☹	☺ 😐 ☹
Speaking	☺ 😐 ☹	☺ 😐 ☹	☺ 😐 ☹	☺ 😐 ☹
My teacher says				

Copyright © by Pearson Education, Ltd.

Diagnostic Pre-Test | Level 2

Name

🎧 Listening

1 **Listen and write.**

1 How many books are there? There are ___ books.
2 How many dogs are there? There is ___ dog.
3 How many apples are there? There are ___ apples.
4 How many hats are there? There are ___ hats.

2 **Look and listen. Circle *T* for *True* or *F* for *False*.**

1 T   F
2 T   F
3 T   F
4 T   F
5 T   F

3 **Listen and write the numbers.**

1 _____   2 _____
3 _____   4 _____
5 _____   6 _____

Diagnostic Pre-Test | Level 2

Name _____

Reading

4 **Read and match. Draw lines.**

1 What's your name?   It's Tuesday.

2 How old are you?   It's my backpack.

3 What's this?   I'm nine years old.

4 What day is it today?   My name is Melanie.

5 **Read and complete. Use the words from the box.**

> brothers   have   I   sister

Nicole: Hi Paul. Look at this picture. This is my family.

Paul: Who's she?

Nicole: She's my _____, and they're my _____.
           1.   2.

Paul: How many brothers do you _____?
                                    3.

Nicole: _____ have three.
           4.

6 **Read, look, and check *yes* or *no*.**

1
She's wearing a skirt, a shirt, and a hat.
☐ yes ☐ no

2
He's wearing a jacket and a T-shirt.
☐ yes ☐ no

3
She's wearing pants, a blouse, and a hat.
☐ yes ☐ no

Level 2 3

Diagnostic Pre-Test | Level 2

Name _____

Writing

7 Look and count. How many?

1. ___ children
2. ___ balls
3. ___ chairs
4. ___ teacher
5. ___ desks

8 Look and write. Use the words from the box.

> He's   It's   She's   They're

1. _____ eating.
2. _____ throwing and catching a ball.
3. The bird is flying. _____ red.
4. _____ singing.

Diagnostic Pre-Test | Level 2

Name _____

9 **Write about your favorite toy.**

_____
_____
_____
_____

10 **Write. Use *has* or *have*.**

1. Does she _____ long hair?
2. My mom _____ four sisters.
3. How many pencils do you _____?
4. They _____ hot dogs and cake on their birthday.
5. What does Melanie _____?

11 **Describe your mom or dad. Write.**

_____
_____
_____
_____

Score: /

Speaking Assessment Prompts | Diagnostic Pre-Test

Speaking Assessment Prompts | Diagnostic Pre-Test | Teacher's Notes

1. Ask the students to describe what they can see in the picture. Point to different people and objects and ask questions: *What is this? Who is this? Is this a…? Can you find a…? Point to a… .* Ask the student to ask you questions about the picture.

2. Ask the student to describe what the children are wearing. Ask questions: *What is this boy wearing?, etc.* Then ask: *What do you like wearing? What do you wear to school? What do you wear at the weekend?*

3. Point to the different activities. Ask the student to describe the activities. Ask questions: *What is this boy/girl doing? Do you like doing this activity? Why do you like doing it? What is your favorite activity? What is your brother's/sister's/friend's favorite activity?*

Practice Test | Unit 1

Name _____

1 Listen and circle.

1 a    b    c

2 a    b    c

2 Circle. Then match and draw lines.

1 They **is** / **are** talking about pictures.

2 He **is** / **are** writing numbers.

3 She **is** / **are** gluing shapes.

4 He **is** / **are** counting pencils.

a
b
c
d

3 Look. Write *is* or *are*.

1 There _____ six rulers.

2 There _____ a backpack.

3 There _____ three erasers.

4 There _____ a desk.

Practice Test | Unit 1   Name

4 Listen and match. Draw lines.

1 markers   1
2 computers   4
3 books   8
4 shapes   19
5 desks   15

5 Look and read. Write *yes* or *no*.

1 One boy is writing letters on the board. _____
2 Three boys are using the computer.   _____
3 One girl is cutting paper.   _____
4 One girl is gluing shapes.   _____
5 The teacher is listening to a story.   _____
6 Two boys are coloring a picture.   _____

Unit Test | Unit 1

Name _____

1) Listen and circle.

1. a  b  c

2. a  b  c

3. a  b  c

2) Look. Write questions and answers.

1. _____
   There are five children.

2. _____
   There is one teacher.

3. How many books are there?
   _____

10 Level 2

Unit Test | Unit 1

Name: _____

3 **Look and write. Use the words from the box.**

| cutting | drawing |
| playing | using |

1 What's the boy doing? He's _____ paper.

2 What are the three children doing? They're _____ a game.

3 What's the teacher doing? He's _____ a picture on the board.

4 What are the two children at the desk doing? They're _____ the computers.

4 **Look and read. Then write ✓ or ✗.**

a  She is listening to a story. ☐

b  She is playing a game. ☐

c  He is counting pencils. ☐

5 **Choose one activity from the box. Write one sentence. Use *he/she is* and *they are*.**

| coloring a picture   listening to a story   playing a computer game |

_____

_____

Score: /

Speaking Assessment Prompts | Unit 1

1

2

 **Speaking Assessment Prompts** | Unit 1 | Teacher's Notes

1. Have the student look at the four pictures. Then prompt the student to tell you about what the children in the picture are doing: *He's using the computer. She's writing her name.* Ask the student what the children are doing: *What's he doing? What are they doing?*.

    Challenge:
   Ask the student to draw a picture of you doing something at your desk in the classroom. Prompt the student to describe the picture and tell what he/she sees.

2. Ask the student to look at the picture. Prompt the student to tell you about at least four different activities that the children are doing, e.g., *This boy / He is…; This girl / She is…; They are… .*

3. Ask the student about school. Say: *Let's talk about your school. Do you like your school? Is your school big or small? Tell me about your classroom. Tell me about your math teacher.*

Level 2

Practice Test | Unit 2

1 Look. Read and check (✓).

1. behind   a  □   b  □   c  □

2. between   a  □   b 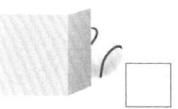 □   c 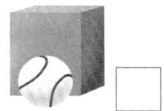 □

3. in front of a 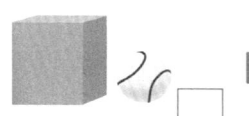 □   b 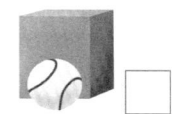 □   c 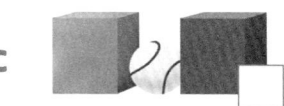 □

4. next to   a  □   b  □   c 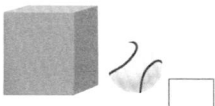 □

2 Listen and complete. Use the words from the box.

| jump rope   play baseball   play basketball   ride a bike |

1. What does Lora like to do?

   She likes to _____.

2. What does Mario like to do?

   He likes to _____.

3. What do Franklin and Elisa like to do?

   They like to _____.

4. What does Lizzie like to do?

   She likes to _____.

Practice Test | Unit 2

Name _____

3 Write the next number.

1 ten, twenty, _____

2 forty, fifty, _____

3 seventy, eighty, _____

4 Listen and number.

a

b

c

d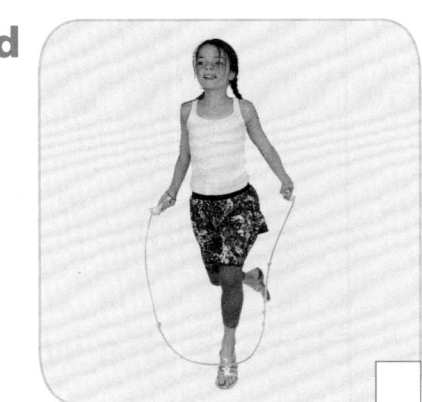

5 What do you like to do? Use one of the words from the box.

> seesaw   slide   swings

_____

Score: /

Level 2   15

Unit Test | Unit 2

Name _____

1. Listen and check (✓).

1. a  b 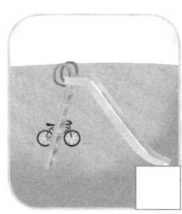 c

2. a 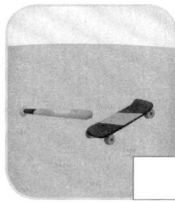 b 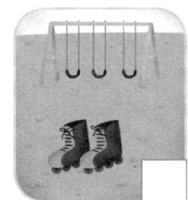 c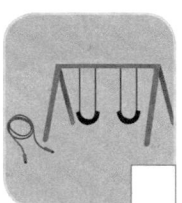

2. Read. Match the words and pictures.

1 kick   a a bike
2 jump   b a ball
3 play   c rope
4 ride   d on the slide

3. Read. Choose the words from the box.

| kick   like (2×)   likes (2×)   play (2×)   ride |

1 Benny _____ to _____ a bike.
2 His mom and dad _____ to _____ games.
3 His brother _____ to _____ a soccer ball.
4 His sisters _____ to _____ basketball.

Unit Test | Unit 2

Name

4 **Match. Draw lines.**

1　fifty　　　　　　　80

2　thirty　　　　　　40

3　ninety　　　　　　50

4　forty　　　　　　30

5　eighty　　　　　　90

5 **What do they like to do? Write sentences.**

1  2  3

1 _____

2 _____

3 _____

6 **Answer the questions.**

1　What do you like to do outside?

_____

2　What do you like to do at school?

_____

Speaking Assessment Prompts | Unit 2

Speaking Assessment Prompts | Unit 2 | Teacher's Notes

1. Ask the student to make a chart of playground activities or general outdoor activities. Draw a basic chart on the board for the student to copy, or pass out a chart that can be filled in. In the first column, have the student write his/her name and the names of two other students. Then have the student fill in headers for at least four columns naming activities (e.g., jump rope, play soccer, ride a bike, etc.). Have the student check the activities he/she likes to do and those that his/her friends like to do. Prompt the student to tell about each activity listed and to ask about the other students: *What do you like to do? What does your friend like to do?*

2. Gather three items used in games or sports, such as a tennis ball, jump rope, and baseball glove. Have the student identify spatial relationships. Place the jump rope behind the ball and ask: *Where is the ball?* Then ask: *Where is the jump rope?* Elicit full sentences, e.g., *The ball is in front of the jump rope. The jump rope is behind the ball.*

 Challenge:
Prompt the student to give you directions for moving the items. Have him/her tell you: *Put the ball next to the baseball glove. Move the glove between the jump rope and the ball.*

3. Have the student look at the picture and find all the pieces of equipment *(jump rope, slide, soccer ball, skates, helmet, bike, skateboard, baseball bat, swing)*. Encourage the student to point to the items as you name them. Say: *Point to the slide.* Ask: *What is he/she doing / playing? What are they doing / playing? Where is the…?* (between/next to/in front of/behind). Ask the student to make sentences about the picture.

Level 2

Practice Test | Unit 3

Name

1 Look. Listen and check (✓) where you find the items.

1 a  b  c

2 a 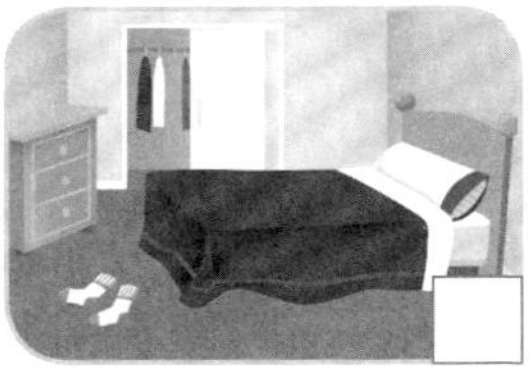  b  c

3 a  b  c

2 Look and read. Write ✓ or ✗.

1 It's in the kitchen.
a  b  c

2 It's in the living room.
a  b  c

3 It's in the bathroom.
a  b  c

Practice Test | Unit 3

3 **Write. Use the names.**

1 Where is my _____ book? **(cousin)**

2 Where is my _____ cell phone? **(uncle)**

3 Where are _____ shoes? **(Henry)**

4 Where is my _____ cup? **(aunt)**

4 **Look, read, and answer. Use the words from the box.**

> between
> in front of   It's
> next to   on

1 Where is her lamp? It's _____ the table.

2 Where are her keys? They're _____ the lamp.

3 Where is her teddy bear? _____ on the bed.

4 Where is the dresser? It's _____ the picture.

5 Where is the bed? It's _____ the dresser and the lamp.

5 **Describe your favorite room. Write two sentences.**

_____

_____

Unit Test | Unit 3

Name _____

1. Listen. Write ✓ or ✗.

1. a   b   c
2. a   b   c
3. a   b   c

2. Read and match. Draw lines.

1. Where is the tub? It's in the   kitchen.
2. Where is the sofa? It's in the   bedroom.
3. Where is the stove? It's in the   bathroom.
4. Where is the closet? It's in the   living room.

3. Write. Use the words from the box.

| aunt   brother   cousins   uncle |

1. My father has a sister. She is my _____.
2. My aunt has two children. They are my _____.
3. My mother has a _____. He is my uncle.
4. My aunt has a husband. He is also my _____.

22 Level 2

Unit Test | Unit 3

Name _____

4 Look and write.

1 _____
2 _____
3 _____
4 _____

5 Look and write. Use *in*, *on*, *behind*, or *in front of*.

a There is a doll _____ the table.

b The girl is skating _____ the tree.

c The skates are _____ the children.

6 Write *It's* or *They're*.

1 Where's the lamp? _____ next to the bed.
2 Where are the new chairs? _____ in the living room.
3 Where's Dad's phone? _____ on the sofa.
4 Where are my sister's glasses? _____ on her dresser.
5 Where are my shoes? _____ under the sink!

7 Where do you do your homework? Describe the room. Write.

_____
_____

Score: /

Speaking Assessment Prompts | Unit 3

24 Level 2

Speaking Assessment Prompts | Unit 3 | Teacher's Notes

1. Ask questions about different rooms in a house and elicit complete sentences for answers. For example, ask: *Where's the refrigerator? (It's in the kitchen.)*

   🎓 **Challenge:**
   Have the student look at the pictures and draw a line between each item to a place in each of the rooms. Check that the student knows the words for each room and each item. Ask: *Where are the skates?* and elicit: *They're in the bedroom.* Encourage him/her to give exact information about where they are: *They're under the chair in the bedroom.*

2. Talk about the student's home. Say: *Let's talk about your home.* Ask: *How many rooms are there? What's in your living room?*

Mastery Test | Units 1–3

Name _____

1 Listen and number.

1 a   b   c

2 a   b   c

3 a   b   c

2 Read and write. Use the words from the box.

> counting   cutting   listening   talking   writing

Donald: Hi, Becky. What are you doing?

Becky: I'm _____ my name. What are you doing?
                    1.

Donald: I'm _____ to you, silly! My friend Paul is
                    2.
_____ to a story.
    3.

Becky: And Stevie's _____ all the pencils.
                            4.

Donald: Wow, look at Maria! She's _____ animals
                                            5.
out of paper. See? That's a cat!

26 Level 2

Mastery Test | Units 1–3

Name _____

3 Look, count, and write how many. Circle *is* or *are*.

1. How many tables are there?

   There **is** / **are** _____ tables in the room.

2. How many doors are there?

   There **is** / **are** _____ door in the room.

3. How many children are there?

   There **is** / **are** _____ children in the room.

4. How many teachers are there?

   There **is** / **are** _____ teacher in the room.

4 Listen and circle.

1. 30 / 40
2. 50 / 70
3. 100 / 10
4. 60 / 50
5. 90 / 80

Level 2

Mastery Test | Units 1–3

Name _____

5 **Look. Answer the questions.**

1 What does she like to do?
_____

2 What do they like to do?
_____

3 What does he like to do?
_____

4 What does he like to do?
_____

5 What does she like to do?
_____

Mastery Test | Units 1–3

Name: _____

6 **Look and check (✓).**

1. The girl is in front of the slide.   a   b   c

2. The seesaw is next to the sandbox.   a   b   c

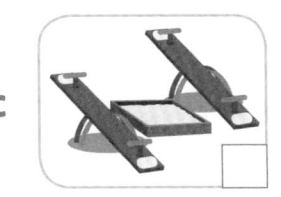

3. The boy is behind the tree.   a   b   c

4. The girl is between the swings.   a   b   c

7 **Read and write *It's* or *They're*.**

1. Where's my sweater? _____ in the closet.
2. Where's my lunch? _____ on the table.
3. Where are Dad's car keys? _____ under the chair.
4. Where are my sister's glasses? _____ next to her phone.
5. Where is my shoe? _____ behind your skates.

Level 2

Mastery Test | Units 1–3

Name _____

8 **Complete the sentences. Use the words from the box.**

> fly   jump   kick   ride

1 I like to _____ a soccer ball.

2 Do you like to _____ kites?

3 My brother and I like to _____ bikes.

4 My friend likes to _____ rope.

9 **Read. Write *like* or *likes*.**

1 The children _____ to skateboard.

2 Morgan _____ to play on the seesaw.

3 His brothers _____ to play basketball.

4 Her sister _____ to play on the slide.

5 My cousin Danny _____ to kick a soccer ball.

6 Anita and Kate _____ to skate.

10 **Choose one activity from the box. Write three sentences about it.**

> drawing pictures   reading books   using the computer

_____

_____

_____

Mastery Test | Units 1–3

Name: _____

11 Look, read, and circle.

1 What's in the kitchen?
   a stove   b bed   c dresser

2 What's in the bathroom?
   a TV   b sofa   c tub

3 What's in the living room?
   a sink   b chair   c closet

4 What's in the bedroom?
   a closet   b sink   c refrigerator

12 Write. Use the names.

1 My uncle is my _____ brother. **(father)**

2 _____ mother is my aunt. **(Benjamin)**

3 Where are _____ keys? **(Gina)**

4 My cousins are my aunt and _____ children. **(uncle)**

5 Where is _____ hat? **(Bobby)**

6 I'm hungry! Where are my _____ cookies? **(aunt)**

Score: /

Practice Test | Unit 4

Name _____

1 **Look. Read and write *yes* or *no*.**

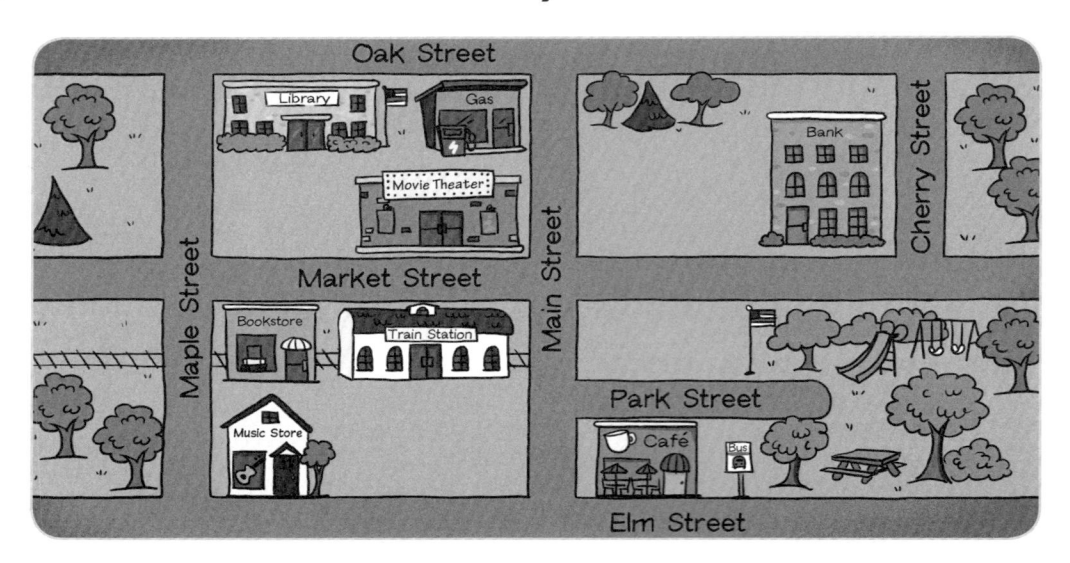

1 There is a movie theater on Market Street. _____

2 There is a movie theater next to the bank. _____

3 There is a music store in front of the bookstore. _____

4 There is a café between the music store and the bus stop. _____

2 **Listen and write. Use the words from the box.**

> between   next to   on (2x)

1 The music store is _____ Elm Street.

2 The movie theater is _____ the gas station and the train station.

3 The computer store is _____ the café.

4 The library is _____ Main Street.

Practice Test | Unit 4

3 **Look and check (✓).**

1. My aunt wants to mail a letter.
   a. Post Office b. Café c. Bookstore

2. My cousins want to eat dinner.
   a. Music Store b. Café c. Gas

3. Julie wants to buy a book.
   a. Bank b. Library c. Bookstore

4. Al wants to have his computer fixed.
   a. Now Showing b. Computer Store c. Music Store

4 **Write *want* or *wants*.**

1. My mom and dad _____ to go to the supermarket near the train station.

2. My sister _____ to shop for shoes in the mall.

3. My brother and I _____ to go to the park.

4. I _____ to see the movie.

5. Maddy _____ to buy popcorn and candy!

5 **Write. What's in your town or city? Write one or two sentences.**

_____

_____

Score: /

Level 2 33

Unit Test | Unit 4

Name _____

1 🔊 **Look and listen. Circle *T* for *True* or *F* for *False*.**

1	T F
2	T F
3	T F
4	T F

2 Look at the map in 1. Answer the questions.

1 Where's the movie theater? _____

2 Is there a bank on Main Street? _____

3 Is there a library on River Street? _____

4 Is there a bus stop on the corner of High Street and Center Street? _____

3 Read and write. Use the words from the box.

> between   near   there isn't   There's   to buy   want

Mimi: Is there a mall _____ your house?
                              1.
Luisa: No, _____. Why? Is there something you
              2.
_____?
   3.
Mimi: I want _____ my mother a book. It's her birthday.
                  4.
Luisa: Oh, no problem! _____ a bookstore near me.
                              5.
It's _____ the supermarket and a restaurant.
        6.
Mimi: Great! Who needs the mall?!

Unit Test | Unit 4

Name _____

4 Read and write ✓ or ✗.

1 The car needs gas. My parents want to stop at a …
   a Post Office   b Gas   c Market

2 I need stamps. I want to go to a …
   a Café   b Movie Theater   c Post Office

3 Mom is hungry. She wants to find a …
   a Café   b Bank   c Library

4 There's a new movie. My brother wants to go to the …
   a Music Store   b Gas   c Movie Theater

5 Read and circle.

1 Andrew **want / wants** to go to the mall.

2 His friends **want / wants** to play baseball in the park.

3 **Andrew / They** want to play now.

4 **Andrew / They** wants to see a movie now.

5 "I **want / wants** to go to the store first," says Andrew.

6 My mom and dad **want / wants** a vacation in Paris!

6 Write. Where is your school? What street is it on? What is it near?

_____

_____

Score: /

Level 2 35

Speaking Assessment Prompts | Unit 4

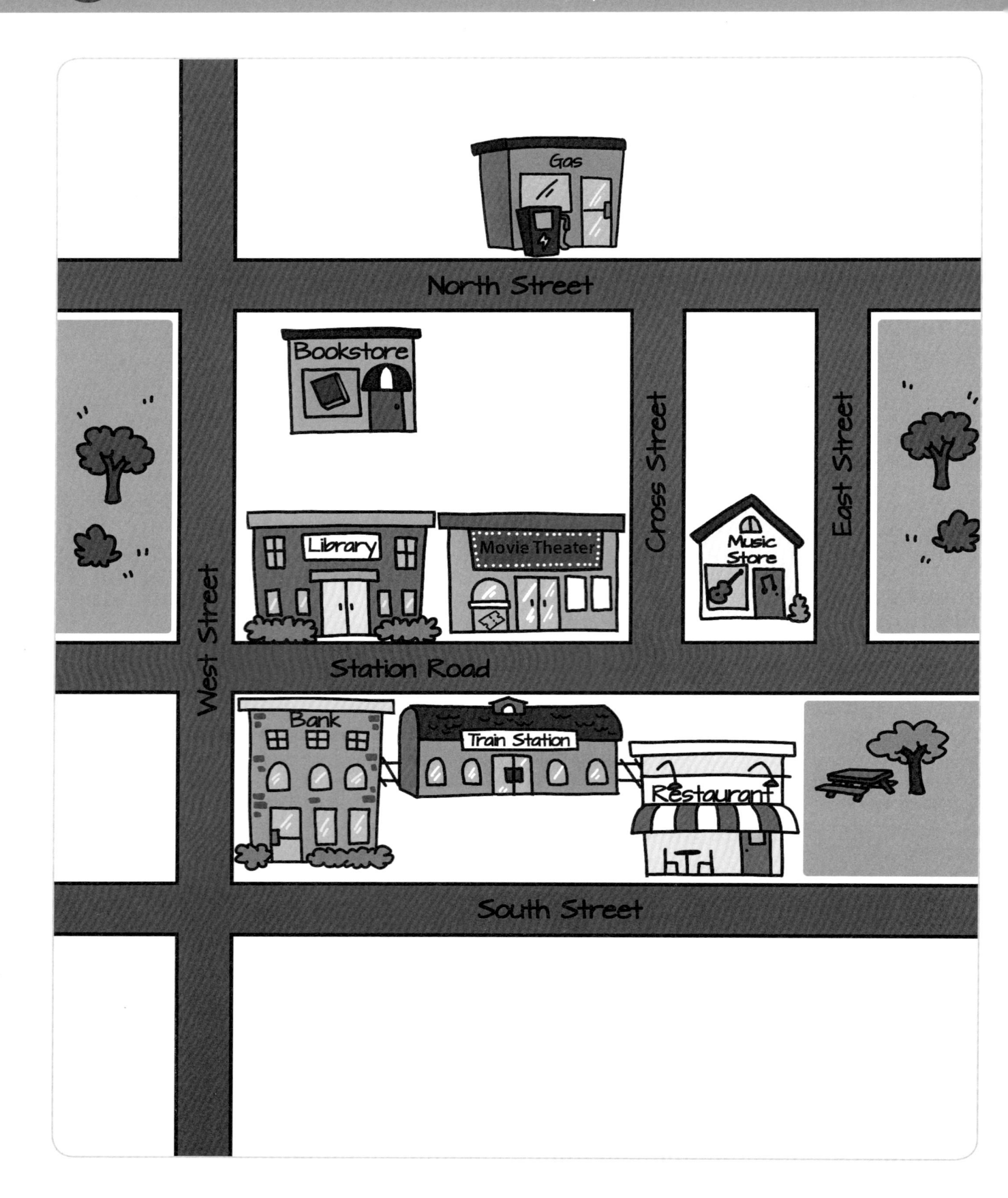

Speaking Assessment Prompts | Unit 4 | Teacher's Notes

1. Have the student look at the map. Ask the student to imagine having just moved to this town. What places does he/she want to go to? Prompt the student to ask you questions: *Is there a movie theater in town? Is there a park in town?* Answer them based on the map.

   Challenge:
   Switch roles. You are new in town. Tell the student something you want or want to do: *I want to eat Mexican food. I want to buy a book. I want to put gas in my car.*, etc. Then ask: *Where should I go?* The student responds by looking at the map and answering, e.g., *There's a restaurant on South Street, but there isn't a café.*

2. Continue using the map. Ask the student to make up a story about two friends, Carmen and Joseph, who spend the day in town. Prompt the student to use third person pronouns and tell what these two "want" to do or where they "want" to go. Prompt the student to make up one or two things that Carmen and Joseph want to do together and at least one thing they want do separately, so that both plural and singular verb forms are used.

3. Say: *Let's talk about your town.* Have the student imagine where he/she lives and encourage him/her to describe what there is in the town. Have the student either describe what there is or ask questions to elicit sentences. If the student needs more support, encourage the student to draw a little map and label a few streets to use as a visual guide.

Practice Test | Unit 5

Name: _____

1 Listen and number. Then check (✓).

☐ vet   a    b    c

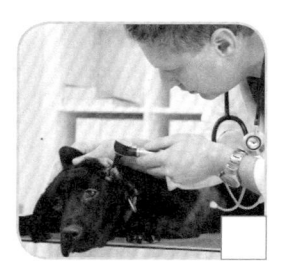

☐ artist   a 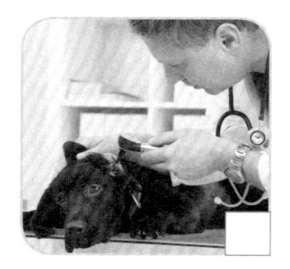   b    c

☐ chef   a    b    c

2 Read and write. Use the words from the box.

> actor   doctor   pilot   teacher

1 A _____ works in a school.

2 Sick people need to see a _____.

3 An _____ plays different roles in movies and plays.

4 A _____ flies an airplane.

38   Level 2

Practice Test | Unit 5

Name

3 Look and read. Check *yes* or *no*.

1 Does he want to be a vet?
☐ yes ☐ no

2 Does she want to be a soccer player?
☐ yes ☐ no

3 Does she want to be a doctor?
☐ yes ☐ no

4 Does he want to be a teacher?
☐ yes ☐ no

4 Read and circle. Then match.

1 What **do** / **does** she want to be?
   She **want** / **wants** to be a dancer.

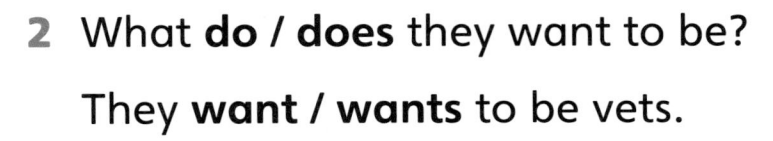

2 What **do** / **does** they want to be?
   They **want** / **wants** to be vets.

3 What **do** / **does** he want to be?
   He **want** / **wants** to be an artist.

4 What **do** / **does** I want to be?
   I **want** / **wants** to be a pilot.

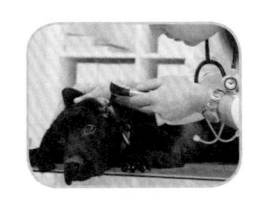

5 Write. What do you want to be? Write one sentence.

_____

Score: /

Level 2   39

Unit Test | Unit 5

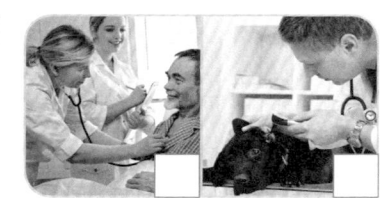

Name _____

1 Listen and check (✓).

1   2   3

2 Write. Use the words from the box. Then match.

doctor   singer   teacher   vet

1 Matthew loves animals. He wants to be a _____.

2 Bella loves to help people. She wants to be a _____.

3 I love music and songs. I want to be a _____.

4 Willis loves children. He wants to be a _____.

3 Write *do* or *does*.

1 What _____ Peter want to be?

2 What _____ you want to be?

3 What _____ the twins want to be?

4 What _____ Amy want to be?

5 What _____ I want to be?

40 Level 2

Unit Test | Unit 5

Name _____

4 **Read, write, and match. Draw lines.**

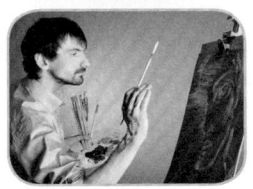

1. I paint pictures and people buy them.
   I am an _____.   a

2. I help people who are very sick.
   I am a _____.   b

3. I run and kick a ball with my team.
   I am a _____.   c

4. I am on stage but I don't speak or sing.
   I am a _____.   d

5 **Read and circle.**

1. What **do / does** your cousin want to be?
2. She **want / wants** to be a firefighter.
3. What **do / does** your brothers want to be?
4. They **want / wants** to be teachers.
5. What **do / does** you want to be?
6. I **want / wants** to be a mail carrier.

6 **What does your friend want to be and why? Write two or three sentences.**

_____

_____

Score: /

Level 2   41

Speaking Assessment Prompts | Unit 5

1

2

42　Level 2

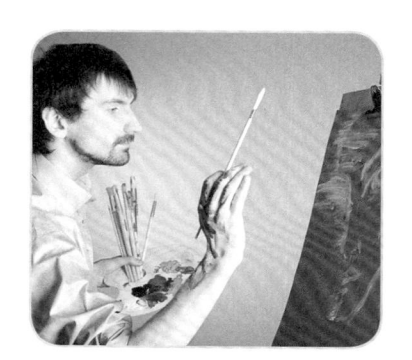

Speaking Assessment Prompts | Unit 5 | Teacher's Notes

1. Ask the student to imagine he/she is having an interview to get a dream job. Have the student say what that job is. Prompt the student to tell something he/she likes to do (e.g., *I like to help animals.*) and then name a job where he/she gets to do what he/she enjoys. Prompt the student to tell why he/she would be good at the job.

   ### 🎓 Challenge:
   Have the student look at the pictures. Ask: *What does she want to do?* (pointing to one of the girls). Invite the student to imagine reasons why they want to do those jobs. Repeat for all four pictures.

2. Show the student pictures of the different jobs. Have the student talk about jobs that other people want to do. Ask the following questions and prompt the student to choose one of the professions in the pictures for each response or encourage the use of other words he/she knows. Remind the student to answer in complete sentences. Ask: *What does your brother want to be? What does your sister want to be? What do your cousins want to be? What does your friend want to be?*

Level 2 43

Practice Test | Unit 6

Name _____

1 **Read. Circle *do* or *does*.**

1. When **do** / **does** she brush her teeth?
2. When **do** / **does** you eat breakfast?
3. When **do** / **does** they go to school?
4. When **do** / **does** Brian get up?

2 **Look and check (✓).**

1. It's seven o'clock.   a ☐   b ☐ 
2. It's four o'clock.   a  ☐   b ☐ 
3. It's twelve o'clock.   a  ☐   b ☐ 
4. It's nine o'clock.   a  ☐   b ☐

3 **Write *do* or *does*. Then write the time.**

1. When _____ you eat lunch? At _____
2. When _____ the movie start? At _____
3. When _____ school end? At _____
4. When _____ your friends do their homework? At _____

44 Level 2

Practice Test | Unit 6

Name: _____

4 **Listen and check (✓). Then answer the questions.**

	go to school	do my homework	feed the cat
Sunday			
Monday			
Tuesday			
Wednesday			
Thursday			
Friday			
Saturday			

1 What does Katie do only on Monday and Saturday?
   _____

2 When does she go to school?
   _____

3 What does Katie do every day of the week?
   _____

4 What do you do every day of the week?
   _____

Katie

5 **Read and circle.**

1 When do **you / Liliana** eat dinner?

2 **I / Emily** get up at 7:00.

3 When do **your father / your brothers** eat breakfast?

4 **He / They** takes a shower at 8:00.

5 When does your **mom / sisters** go to bed?

6 **What / When** time is it?

Score: /

Unit Test | Unit 6

Name _____

1. Listen and check (✓). Write the time.

1 He gets up at
   _____.   a   b

2 School starts at
   _____.   a   b

3 They eat lunch at
   _____.   a   b

4 School ends at
   _____.   a   b

5 He goes to bed at
   _____.   a   b

2. Number in order.

☐ At seven o'clock I eat breakfast.

☐ I brush my teeth after dinner at seven o'clock.

☐ I do my homework before bed at nine o'clock.

☐ In the morning I get up at six o'clock.

☐ I take a shower at eight o'clock in the morning.

☐ I eat lunch at twelve o'clock.

46 Level 2

Unit Test | **Unit 6**   Name

3 **Circle *T* for *True* or *F* for *False* for you.**

1 I go to school every day.   T   F
2 I go to bed every day.   T   F
3 I have cake every day at 10:00. T   F
4 I get up every day.   T   F

4 **Look and answer. Write complete sentences.**

1 What time does she go to bed?
_____

2 When does she take a bath?
_____

3 What time do they watch TV?
_____

4 When do they ride their bikes?
_____

5 **Write sentences. Answer the questions.**

1 When do you eat breakfast on school days?
_____

2 When do you start school in the morning?
_____

6 **Write. What do you do on Saturday mornings?**

_____

Score: /

Level 2   47

Speaking Assessment Prompts | Unit 6

1

1:00 2:00 3:00 4:00 5:00 6:00

7:00 8:00 9:00 10:00 11:00 12:00

2

48 Level 2

Speaking Assessment Prompts | Unit 6 | Teacher's Notes

1. Have the student draw a picture showing at least three things to do every day. Ask the student to tell about these things in the order that he/she does them. Have the student refer to the pictures of clocks to help him/her choose different times.

   🎓 **Challenge:**
   Ask the student to select the thing he/she likes to do the most and give one or two reasons why he/she likes this particular activity.

2. Prompt the student to talk about different times of the day. Fold a piece of paper into three sections and label the sections *Morning*, *Afternoon*, and *Evening*. Have the student list at least two activities that are sometimes or often (but not always) done for each section, along with the approximate time that the activity takes place. Using the chart, the student tells you about each activity. For example, under *Evening*, the student writes *5 o'clock, help with dinner*. He/She says, *Some days, at 5 o'clock, I help my mom make dinner*. Now have the student look at the pictures and ask a question for each one. Ask: *When does school start? (It starts at eight o'clock.)*

3. Tell the student you are going to talk about his/her day. Say: *Let's talk about a Monday and a Saturday.* Ask questions to elicit differences. Ask: *When do you get up on Monday? And Saturday?* or encourage him/her to talk about the days independently without prompts.

   🎓 **Challenge:**
   Invite the student to find out from his/her best friend what time he/she does different things. Then ask about the friend's day. Ask: *When does he/she get dressed?*

Level 2 49

Mastery Test | Units 4–6

Name _____

1 🎧 **Listen. Look. Circle T for True or F for False.**

1. T   F
2. T   F
3. T   F
4. T   F

2 **Read and write. Use the words from the box.**

| between | near | There isn't |
| There's | to buy | want |

Lois: I _____ a good book to read.
                    1.

Mark: Do you want _____ a book? _____ a big
                             2.   3.
bookstore in the mall.

Lois: Great. Let's go! Is there a bus stop _____ here?
                                                                  4.

Mark: Yes, it's _____ my house and the corner.
                          5.
We can get a hot dog on the way home. _____
                                                                            6.
any food in this house!

50 Level 2

Mastery Test | Units 4–6

Name

3 Look. Read and answer.

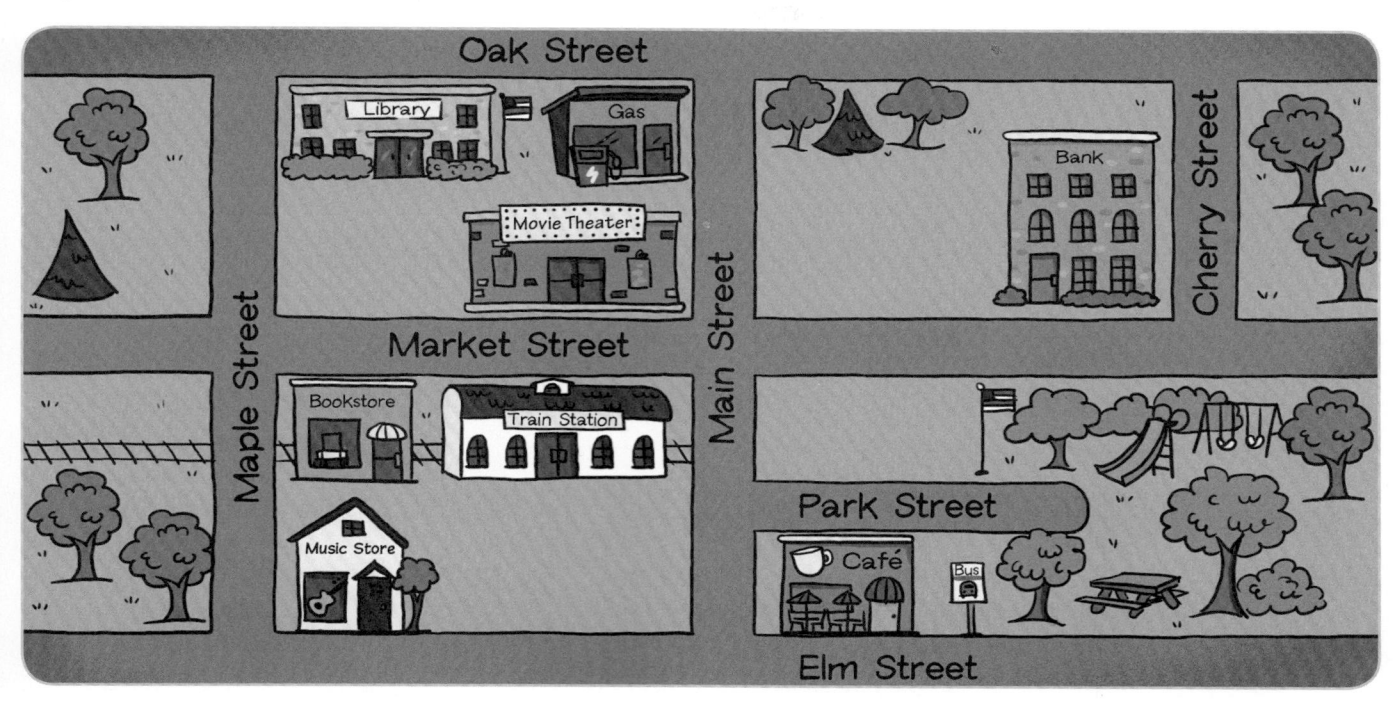

1 Is there a movie theater on Elm Street?

   _____

2 Is there a bank on Market Street?

   _____

3 Is there a bookstore on Maple Street?

   _____

4 Is there a café on Cherry Street?

   _____

Level 2

Mastery Test | Units 4–6   Name

4 Read and complete.

1 I _____ to go to the movies. **(want, wants)**

2 _____ wants to fly kites in the park. **(My friends, My friend)**

3 _____ want to go to the computer store. **(My brother, My brothers)**

4 My mom _____ me to mail a letter. **(want, wants)**

5 Write sentences and answer.

1 Where's the café?

    _____

2 Where are the post office and the computer store?

    _____

3 Where's the movie theater?

    _____

Mastery Test | Units 4–6

Name: _____

6 Listen and number.

7 Write *do* or *does*.

1. What _____ Peter want to be?
2. What _____ you want to be?
3. What _____ your cousins want to be?
4. What _____ Amy want to be?
5. What _____ I want to be?

8 Write. Use the words from the box.

| actor   artist   chef   teacher |

1. Kate loves to cook. _____
2. Eddie likes to help kids learn new things. _____
3. Mira loves to perform in plays. _____
4. Michel loves to paint. _____

Level 2   53

Mastery Test | Units 4–6

Name _____

9 Listen and write ✓ or ✗. Then write.

1 It's _____.

2 It's _____.

3 It's _____.

4 It's _____.

5 It's _____.

10 Read and match. Draw lines.

1 They get up   lunch at school.

2 She takes   their homework at 4:00.

3 I brush   school at 8:00.

4 Leslie goes to   my teeth before bed.

5 My friends eat   a shower in the morning.

6 Peter and Kim do   at 6:00.

54 Level 2

Mastery Test | Units 4–6

Name

11. Listen and match. Draw lines.

1 Jason   a

2 Mike   b

3 Karen   c

4 Elaine   d

5 Sally   e

12. Write.

What is one thing you do every day?

_____

What do you want to be? Why?

_____

_____

Score: /

Level 2   55

Practice Test | Unit 7

Name _____

1. Listen and check (✓).

1. a 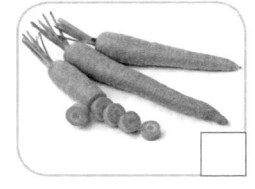 b  c 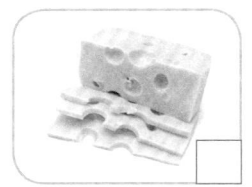
2. a  b  c 
3. a  b  c 
4. a  b  c

2. Read and write. Answer the questions.

1. Do you like spaghetti?
   Yes, _____.

2. Do you like water?
   No, _____.

3. Does Olivia like yogurt?
   No, _____.

4. Do your classmates like potatoes?
   Yes, _____.

5. Does Mr. Cruz like strawberries?
   No, _____.

3. Write. What are your favorite foods for breakfast?

_____

_____

56 Level 2

Practice Test | Unit 7

4 Complete the words. Use a, e, i, o, or u.

1 t ___ m ___ t ___ ___ s
2 ch ___ ___ s ___
3 p ___ t ___ t ___ ___ s
4 c ___ rr ___ ts
5 p ___ n ___ ___ ppl ___
6 ch ___ ck ___ n

5 Look at the chart. Answer the questions.

mangoes   cookies   cheese   fries   burgers   bananas

	Janice	Bruce	Lena
mangoes	✓		
burgers			✓
cheese		✓	

	Janice	Bruce	Lena
bananas	✓		
fries			✓
cookies		✓	

1 What does Janice want?

   She _____ _____ and _____.

2 What does Bruce want?

   He _____ _____ and _____.

3 What does Lena want?

   She _____ _____ and _____.

Score: /

Level 2   57

Unit Test | Unit 7

Name _____

1 **Look and write. Then listen and write Y for Yes or N for No.**

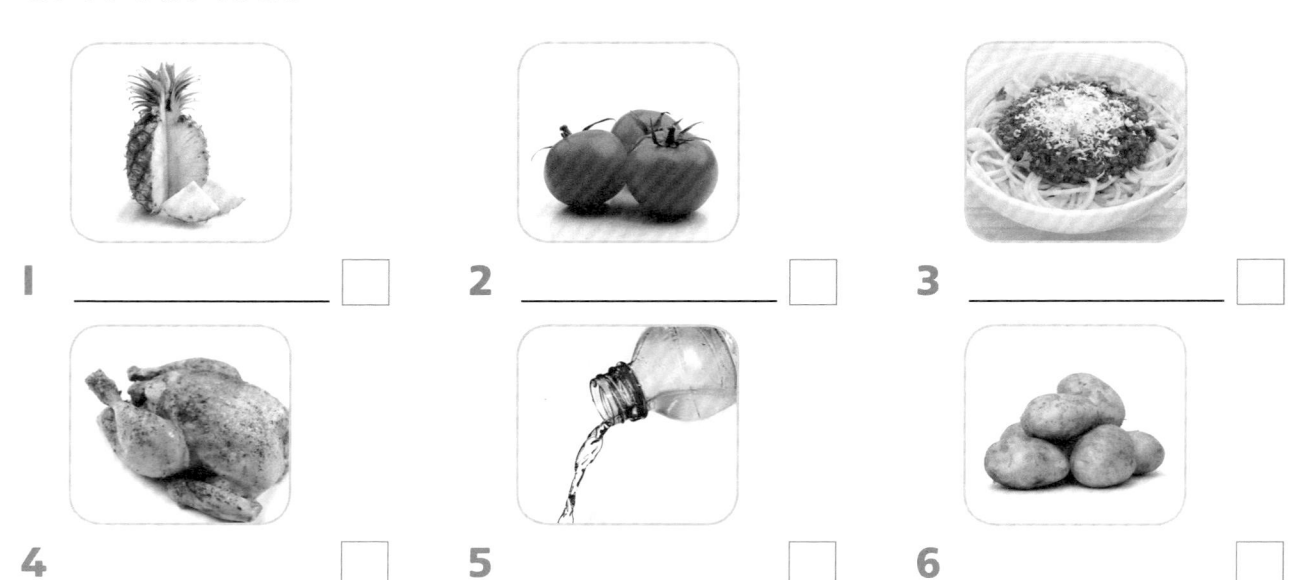

1 _____ ☐   2 _____ ☐   3 _____ ☐

4 _____ ☐   5 _____ ☐   6 _____ ☐

2 **Look. Write the questions.**

1 _____?

Yes, they like corn.

2 _____?

Yes, she likes strawberries.

3 **Complete the questions. Use the correct form of *do*.**

1 What _____ you want to eat?

2 _____ your grandpa like cheese?

3 What _____ your friend want to eat?

4 _____ you and Dina want some pie?

58 Level 2

Unit Test | Unit 7

Name _____

4 **Write. Use the words from the box.**

> apple   do   don't   fruit   potatoes

Milo: Dad, do you like vegetables?

Dad: Yes, I _____ . I like _____ and carrots.
  1.   2.
Do you like vegetables?

Milo: No, I _____ . I like _____ . I eat an
  3.   4.
_____ and two oranges every day!
  5.

5 **Look and read. Then write ✓ or ✗.**

1 strawberries

2 carrots

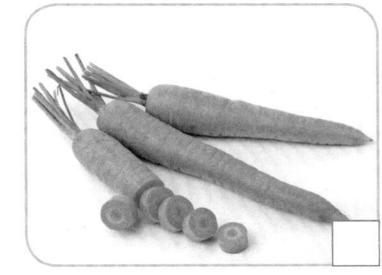

3 lemonade

4 yogurt

6 **Write. What is your favorite meal? What foods do you want?**

_____

Score: /

Speaking Assessment Prompts | Unit 7

Speaking Assessment Prompts | Unit 7 | Teacher's Notes

1. Have the student draw a picture of a table with different foods on it. Encourage the student to include at least five foods he/she likes and two foods he/she doesn't like. Point to specific foods in the student's drawing and ask, *Do you like [apples/hamburgers/carrots]?* When the student has a negative response, prompt him/her to also make a statement about something he/she does like. (e.g., *I don't like carrots, I like potatoes.*) Then ask the same questions about the student's family or friends: *Does your mom/brother/best friend like hot dogs? Do your friends like cake?*

2. Have the student look at the picture. Say: *It's the school fair. This is the food stall. What food do you want?* Have the student say what food he/she wants. Then say: *It's 12 o'clock. It's lunchtime.* Ask specific questions: *Do you want some chicken or some spaghetti?*

🎓 Challenge:
Have the student tell about a holiday/celebration when his/her family eats special foods. Prompt the student to describe the meal or one special dish eaten on that day.

3. Say: *Let's talk about your favorite foods.* Ask the student what his/her favorite fruit is and then repeat for vegetables and snacks.

Practice Test | Unit 8

Name _____

1 Write the words.

1  _____ 2  _____ 3 _____

4  _____ 5  _____ 6 _____

2 Read and circle.

1 Can elephants climb trees? **No, it can't. / No, they can't.**

2 Can a toucan fly? **Yes, it can. / Yes, they can.**

3 Can a monkey hang from a tree? **No, it can't. / Yes, it can.**

4 Can lions run fast? **No, they can't. / Yes, they can.**

3 Read and match. Draw lines.

1 A monkey can   jump. They have pouches.

2 Polar bears can   fly and talk. It has sharp claws.

3 Kangaroos can   swim. They are strong.

4 A parrot can   climb trees and hang by its tail.

Practice Test | Unit 8

Name _____

4 **Listen and complete the sentences. Then number.**

1 A _____ climb a tree.

2 An _____ talk.

3 A _____ run fast.

4 A _____ fly.

5 A _____ fly.

6 A _____ swim.

5 **What is your favorite animal? Write two sentences.**

_____

_____

Score: /

Level 2   63

Unit Test | Unit 8

Name _____

1. Look and write. What am I? Write ✓ or ✗.

1. I can eat a lot. I can't jump. I am a _____.
   - a 
   - b 
   - c

2. I can't climb a tree, but I can eat its leaves. I am a _____.
   - a 
   - b 
   - c

2. Listen and check (✓).

1. a  b 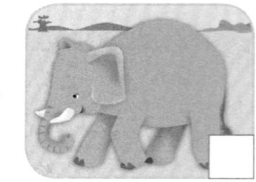 c 
2. a  b  c 
3. a  b  c 
4. a  b 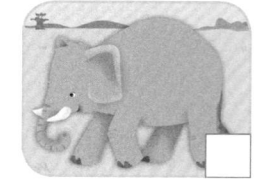 c

3. Number in order.

____ Hi, Linda! What's that?

____ Yes, it can.

____ I like its beak. Can it fly?

____ Hey, Ben! It's a toucan.

Unit Test | Unit 8

Name _____

4 **Answer the questions. Write sentences. Use *can* or *can't*.**

1 Can a zebra climb a tree? _____
2 Can toucans swim? _____
3 Can a peacock fly? _____
4 Can giraffes hang from trees? _____
5 Can a cheetah talk? _____

5 **Fill in the categories. Use all the animals in the box. You can use animals more than once.**

> cheetah   elephant   giraffe   hippo   kangaroo
> monkey   peacock   polar bear   snake   zebra

Can fly	Can climb	Can jump

Can swim	Can run fast

6 **Some animals are dangerous. Pick one. Write two sentences about it.**

_____

_____

Score: /

Speaking Assessment Prompts | Unit 8

66 Level 2

Speaking Assessment Prompts | Unit 8 | Teacher's Notes

1. Have the student look at the pictures of different animals. Ask the student to point out an animal they like. Ask questions about the different features of the animal: *Does a kangaroo have a short tail? (No, it has a long tail.)* Have the student pick a second animal and repeat the process.

   ### 🎓 Challenge:
   Have the student tell you what kind of habitat each of these animals lives in.

2. Ask the student to play a guessing game where the teacher does the guessing. Have the student imagine he/she is one of the animals from this unit. Without telling you what animal he/she is, have the student make statements about what he/she can or can't do *(I can climb trees. I can hang from my tail.)* and/or what features he/she has *(I don't have claws.)*.

3. Have the student look at the pictures of the animals again. Ask questions about each animal, using *can* and *like*: *Can a hippo jump? Do you like hippos?* Alternate using singular and plural questions *(Can a giraffe…? Can elephants…?)*.

Practice Test | Unit 9

Name _____

1 🎧 Listen and check (✓).

1 Pam   a June b July c February

2 Your family   a October b August c April

3 Eric   a October b December c November

4 Your friends a May b February c June

2 Write the next month.

1 June, July, August, _____

2 September, October, November, _____

3 February, March, April, _____

3 Match. Draw lines.

1 In the winter I always   in the fall.

2 I love the summer because   the spring.

3 My school starts   skate on ice.

4 April is in   it's my birthday!

68 Level 2

Practice Test | Unit 9

Name: _____

4 **Write *always* or *never*.**

1. Do you have cake on your birthday?

   Yes, I _____ have cake and ice cream on my birthday.

2. Do you ever have pie on a holiday?

   Yes, I _____ have pie and ice cream on Thanksgiving.

3. Do you ever play basketball?

   No, I don't. I _____ play basketball. I like soccer.

5 **Write.**

1. What do you do in October?

   _____

2. What do you do in December?

   _____

3. What do you do in May?

   _____

4. What do you do in July?

   _____

6 **Read and write.**   December   September   August

_____   _____   _____

Score: /

Level 2 **69**

Unit Test | Unit 9

Name _____

1. Listen and check (✓).

1 a ☐ b ☐   2 a ☐ b ☐

3 a ☐ b ☐   4 a ☐ b ☐

2. Write *always* or *never*.

1 Does your school end in June this year?

Yes, my school _____ ends in June.

2 Do you like to eat strawberries in the summer?

No, I _____ eat strawberries!

3 Does your family go on vacation in August?

Yes, we _____ go to visit my grandparents.

4 Do your grandparents ever visit you?

Yes, they _____ visit us for New Year's.

3. Read and circle.

1 What **do / does** your cousin do all summer?

2 What **do / does** you do in the fall?

3 What **do / does** your friends do in winter?

4 **Do / Does** you do anything for spring vacation?

Unit Test | Unit 9

Name _____

4 Read and write. Answer the questions.

> January   February   March   April   May   June   July
> August   September   October   November   December

1. What month is it now? _____
2. When is your birthday? _____
3. When do you finish school this year? _____
4. What month is very cold where you live? _____
5. What month is very hot where you live? _____

5 Read and write. Use the words from the box.

> always   May   month   summer   the

1. My friend Rick has a birthday in _____.
2. What do you do in _____ spring?
3. We never do homework in the _____.
4. I _____ have a birthday party.
5. What's your favorite _____?

6 What's your favorite month? Write three things you like about it.

_____
_____
_____

Score: /

Level 2

Speaking Assessment Prompts | Unit 9

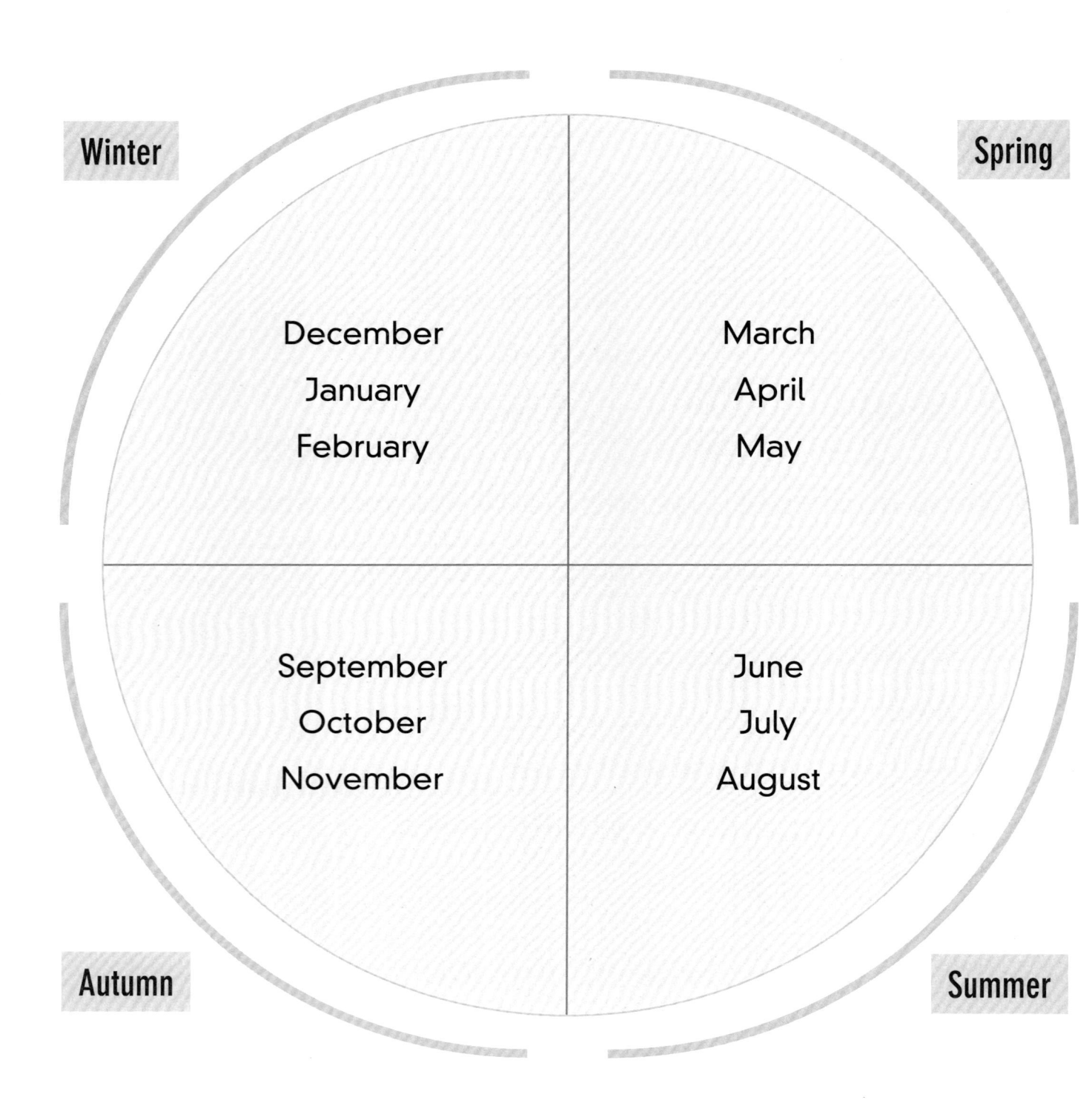

Winter
- December
- January
- February

Spring
- March
- April
- May

Autumn
- September
- October
- November

Summer
- June
- July
- August

Speaking Assessment Prompts | Unit 9 | Teacher's Notes

1. Write the name of each month on a square of different colored paper and keep them mixed up in a basket or bag. Have the student empty the basket on the table and arrange the months in order while saying each name. Ask the student to point to his/her birthday month. Have the student tell you: *My birthday is in [name of month].* Ask: *Is it in the spring, summer, fall, or winter?* Ask about the birthdays of other family members: *What month is your mom's/dad's birthday?* If there are siblings, ask about their birthdays.

2. Have the student look at the months on their page. Have the student pick out one month at random. Ask: *What do you do in [name of month]?* Prompt the student to tell you something different he/she does in this month *(It's the month we celebrate [name of holiday]. It's the month we moved to town. It's the month school starts.).* If the student can think of nothing special, prompt with specific questions, e.g., *Does your grandmother visit you in May?*

🎓 Challenge:

Ask: *What month do you dislike the most?* Have the student tell you about his/her least favorite month. Prompt the student to give at least one reason. *(It's boring. / It's too cold to ride my bike! / School starts! / There aren't any holidays!)* Then repeat for the student's favorite month.

3. Ask specific questions about different months. Ask: *Do you go on vacation in November? Do you play in the park in July? When do you…? What do you do in…?*

Level 2   73

Mastery Test | Units 7–9   Name

1. Listen and check (✓).

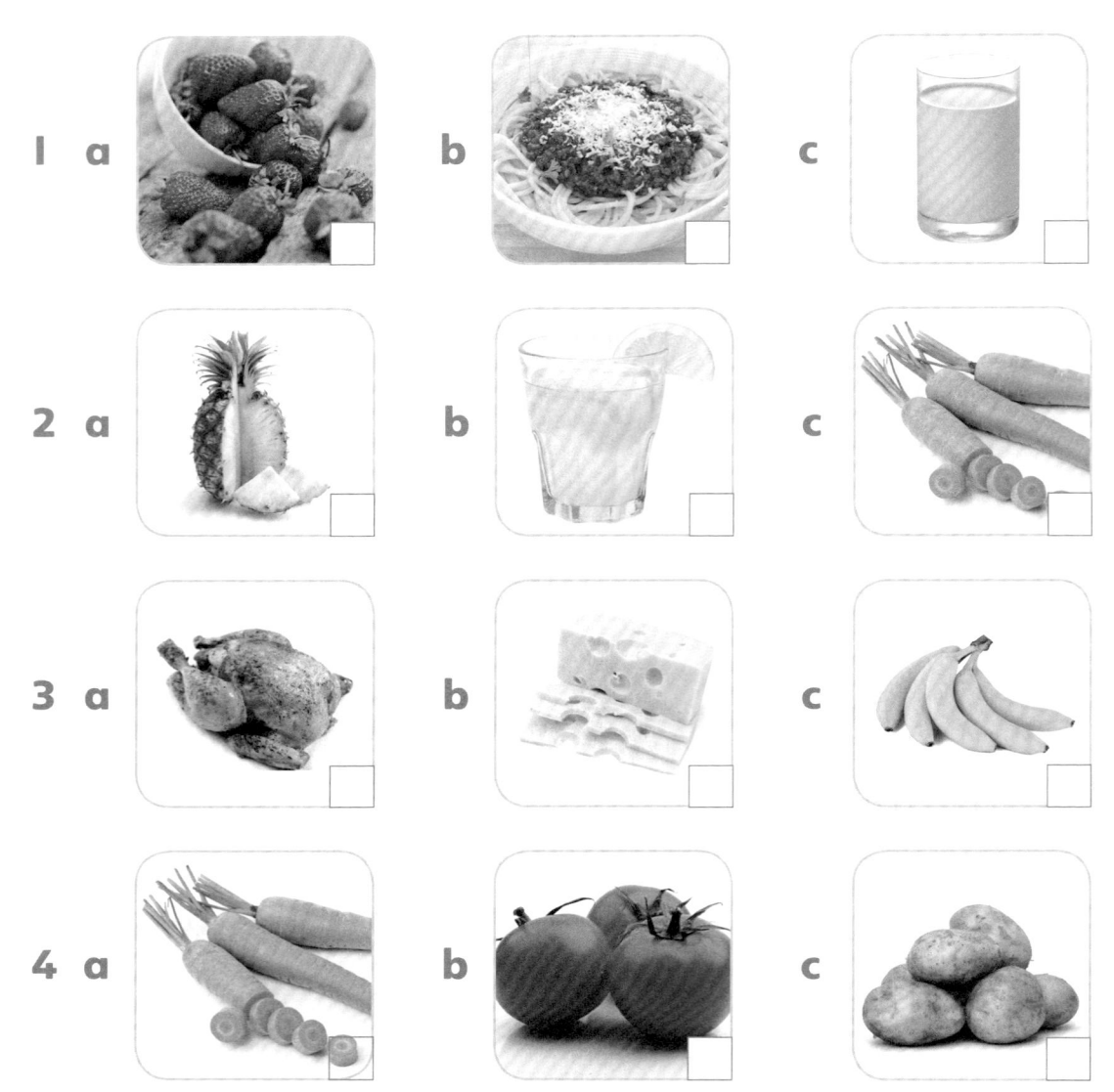

1. a b c

2. a b c

3. a b c

4. a b c

2. Circle *do* or *does*.

1. **Do** / **Does** you like cookies?
2. What **do** / **does** your mom want to drink?
3. What **do** / **does** your parents want to eat?
4. What movie **do** / **does** your friend want to see?

Mastery Test | Units 7–9   Name _____

3 **Complete the dialog. Use the words from the box.**

> carrots   do   like   pineapple
> potatoes   strawberries   want

Frankie: Do you like vegetables?

Rajah: Yes, I _____. I like _____ and
1.   2.
_____. Do you _____ fruit?
3.   4.

Frankie: Yes! I like _____ and _____.
5.   6.

Rajah: I'm hungry! What do you _____ for dinner?
7.

Frankie: Let's have pizza!

4 **Look at the chart. Answer the questions.**

	Gary		Inez	
	Like	Don't Like	Like	Don't Like
bananas	✓		✓	
corn		✓		✓
yogurt	✓		✓	
carrots		✓		✓
chicken	✓			✓

1 Does Inez like bananas? _____

2 Does Gary like carrots? _____

3 Does Inez like chicken? _____

4 Do Inez and Gary like corn? _____

5 Do Gary and Inez like yogurt? _____

Level 2

Mastery Test | Units 7–9

Name

5 **Read and check (✓).**

1 hippo   a    b    c

2 cheetah   a    b    c

3 kangaroo   a    b    c

4 zebra   a    b    c

6 **Read and answer. Circle *T* for *True* or *F* for *False*.**

1 Elephants can't fly.   T   F

2 Kangaroos can't jump.   T   F

3 Giraffes can climb trees.   T   F

4 Lions can run fast.   T   F

Mastery Test | Units 7–9

Name _____

7 **Complete the questions. Then answer the questions. Use *can* or *can't*.**

1 _____ cheetahs run?

   _____

2 _____ a polar bear swim?

   _____

3 _____ zebras climb trees?

   _____

4 _____ parrots fly?

   _____

5 _____ a kangaroo hang by its tail?

   _____

8 **Look and write. Use the words from the box.**

| a kangaroo   a monkey   a parrot   an elephant |

1 I can hang by my tail in a tree. I am _____.
2 I'm big and I have ears and a trunk. I am _____.
3 I can jump and I have a pouch. I am _____.
4 I can fly and I have sharp claws. I am _____.

Level 2 77

Mastery Test | Units 7–9

Name:

9 Listen and check (✓).

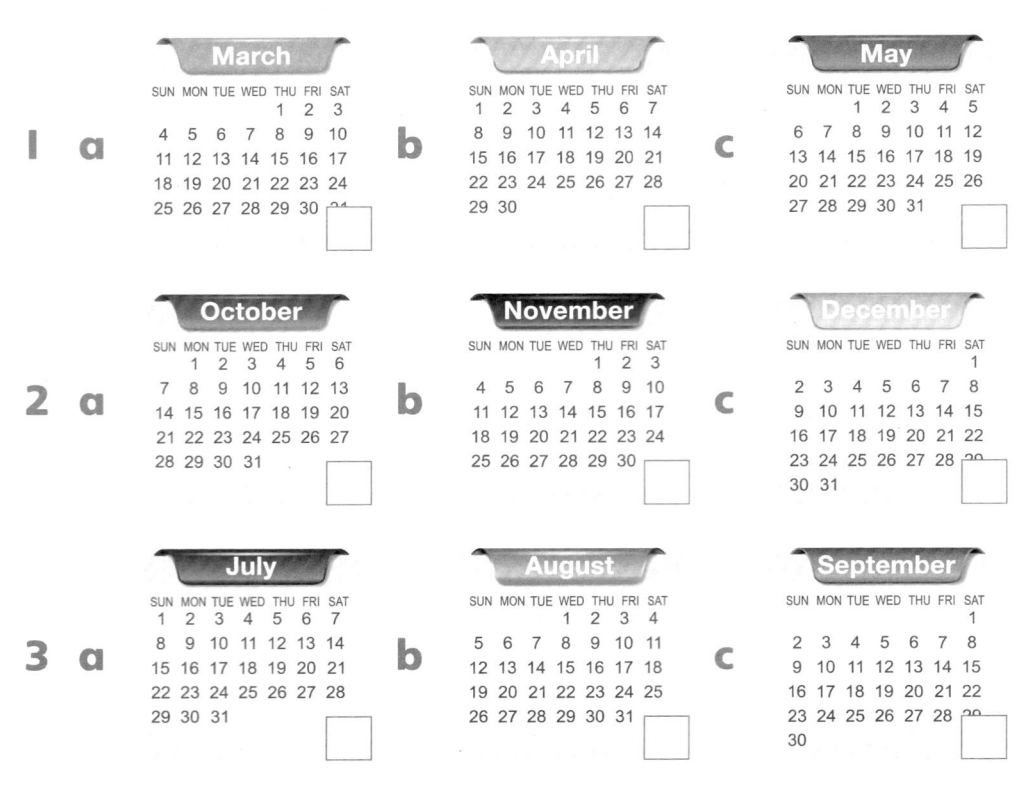

1 a. March b. April c. May

2 a. October b. November c. December

3 a. July b. August c. September

10 Listen and match. Draw lines.

1 February   birthday

2 August   swimming

3 October   winter vacation

4 July   cousins' visit

11 Write. What is your favorite time of the year? Is it summer, fall, winter, or spring? Tell three things you like about it and what you do.

_____

_____

_____

Mastery Test | Units 7–9   Name

12 **Read. Circle *always* or *never*.**

1 Does your school end in June this year?

Yes, my school **always / never** ends in June.

2 Do you make lemonade in the summer?

No, I **always / never** make lemonade at any time of the year!

3 Do you have a cake on your birthday?

Yes, I **always / never** have a cake on my birthday.

4 Does your family go to the lake on weekends?

No, we **always / never** go to the lake.

13 **Listen and write.**

Stella: What do you do in _____?
                                              1.

Peter: I like to _____ on the ice. Do you go on
                          2.
vacation in the winter?

Stella: No, I _____. We never go away in the
                       3.
_____. My _____ month is July.
      4.   5.

Peter: Really? I love July, too.

Score: /   Level 2   **79**

Final Exam | Level 2

Name

🎧 Listening

1. Listen and number.

2. Listen and check (✓).

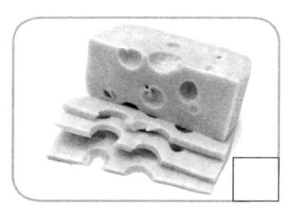

1.

2.

3.

4.

3. Listen and write the number.

1 ____   2 ____   3 ____   4 ____   5 ____

80 Level 2

Final Exam | Level 2

Name

📖 Reading

4 **Read and match. Draw lines.**

1 Where is the tub?   It's in the kitchen.

2 Where is the sofa?   It's in the bedroom.

3 Where is the stove?   It's in the bathroom.

4 Where is the bed?   It's in the living room.

5 **Look and read. Circle *T* for *True* or *F* for *False*.**

1 The movie theater is on Castle Road.   T   F

2 The café is between the supermarket and the library.   T   F

3 There's a bank on Park Avenue.   T   F

4 Where's the post office? It's on Beech Avenue.   T   F

5 The train station is on the corner of High Street
   and London Road.   T   F

Level 2   81

Final Exam | Level 2

Name

📖 Reading

6 Match. Draw lines.

1 I wake up at seven o'clock in the morning.

2 She plays soccer at three o'clock in the afternoon.

3 He eats dinner at six o'clock.

4 My parents watch the news at nine o'clock.

a

b

c

d

7 Match. Draw lines.

1 Can a cheetah run fast?   No, it can't.

2 Can a snake fly?   Yes, it can.

3 Can giraffes talk?   Yes, they can.

4 Can polar bears swim?   No, they can't.

8 Look and read. Write ✓ or ✗.

1 This is a peacock.

2 She's an athlete.

3 These are burgers.

4 This is a bus stop.

82 Level 2

Final Exam | Level 2

Writing

9 **Answer the questions. Write sentences.**

1 2 3 4

1 What does she like to do? _____

2 What does she like to do? _____

3 What does he like to do? _____

4 What do they like to do? _____

10 **Read and write. Use the words from the box.**

> bookstore   computer store   post office   restaurant

1 Mark wants to buy a computer game. He goes to a _____.

2 My cousin needs to mail a letter. He goes to the _____.

3 Mom is hungry. She wants to go to a _____.

4 I want to buy a book. I want to go to a _____.

Final Exam | Level 2

Name _____

11 **Read the answers. Write the questions.**

1 _____
   She wants to be a dancer.

2 _____
   I want to be a vet.

3 _____
   He wants to be an actor.

4 _____
   They want to be mail carriers.

12 **Write.**

1 What is your favorite animal? What can it do?
   Write two sentences.
   _____
   _____

2 What do you do every day? What do you do on Sundays?
   _____
   _____

3 Choose one month you like and one you don't like. Write sentences.
   _____
   _____

Score: /

Speaking Assessment Prompts | Final Exam

Level 2   85

Speaking Assessment Prompts | Final Exam | Teacher's Note

1. Have the student describe what they can see in the picture. Point to different rooms in the house. Ask: *What room is this? What furniture can you find in a kitchen? ...in a bathroom? ...in a living room? ...in a bedroom?*, etc. Ask: *What furniture is in your bedroom / living room?*, etc.

2. Have the student look at the other things in the picture. Ask: *What are the children doing? What is he/she doing? What do you like doing? What do you like doing in winter / summer?*

3. Ask the student: *What food is the family eating for their picnic? What is your favorite food? What food do you have on a picnic? Do you like…? Do your parents like…? What food do you have for special occasions?*

Answer Key and Audioscript | Level 2

Diagnostic Pre-Test

1. **1.** 11, **2.** 1, **3.** 15, **4.** 6

   🎧 2 1. How many books are there?
   There are eleven books.
   2. How many dogs are there?
   There is one dog.
   3. How many apples are there?
   There are fifteen apples.
   4. How many hats are there?
   There are six hats.

2. **1.** T, **2.** F, **3.** F, **4.** T, **5.** T

   🎧 3 1. The frog is jumping.
   2. The cat is eating.
   3. The duck is flying.
   4. The cat is sleeping.
   5. The dog is running.

3. **1.** 19, **2.** 8, **3.** 20, **4.** 12, **5.** 15, **6.** 13

   🎧 4 1. nineteen
   2. eight
   3. twenty
   4. twelve
   5. fifteen
   6. thirteen

4. **1.** My name is Melanie.
   2. I'm nine years old.
   3. It's my backpack.
   4. It's Tuesday.

5. **1.** sister, **2.** brothers, **3.** have, **4.** I

6. **1.** no, **2.** yes, **3.** no

7. **1.** 4, **2.** 2, **3.** 6, **4.** 1, **5.** 3

8. **1.** He's, **2.** They're, **3.** It's, **4.** She's

10. **1.** have, **2.** has, **3.** have, **4.** have, **5.** have

Unit 1 Practice Test

1. **1.** b, **2.** a

   🎧 5 1. What's she doing?
   She's listening to music.
   2. What's he doing?
   He's coloring a picture.

2. **1.** are, c, **2.** is, d, **3.** is, b, **4.** is, a

3. **1.** are, **2.** is, **3.** are, **4.** is

4. **1.** 8, **2.** 1, **3.** 19, **4.** 4, **5.** 15

   🎧 6 1. How many markers are there?
   There are eight markers in the box.
   2. How many computers are there?
   There is one computer in this classroom.
   3. How many books are there?
   There are nineteen books in the bookstore.
   4. How many shapes are there?
   There are four shapes in the picture.
   5. How many desks are there?
   There are fifteen desks in the classroom.

5. **1.** yes, **2.** no, **3.** yes, **4.** yes, **5.** no, **6.** no

Unit 1 Unit Test

1. **1.** a, **2.** c, **3.** a

   🎧 7 He's cutting shapes for a picture.
   They're playing soccer.
   She's playing a game.

2. **1.** How many children are there?
   2. How many teachers are there?
   3. There's one book.

3. **1.** cutting, **2.** playing, **3.** drawing, **4.** using

4. **1.** ✗, **2.** ✓, **3.** ✓

Level 2 **87**

Answer Key and Audioscript | Level 2

Unit 2 Practice Test

I. 1. b, 2. a, 3. b, 4. c

2. 1. play basketball, 2. ride a bike, 3. jump rope, 4. play baseball

(8) 1. What does Lora like to do?
     She likes to play basketball.
   2. What does Mario like to do?
     He likes to ride a bike.
   3. What do Franklin and Elisa like to do?
     They like to jump rope.
   4. What does Lizzie like to do?
     She likes to play baseball.

3. 1. thirty, 2. sixty, 3. ninety

4. a. 2, b. 1, c. 4, d. 3

(9) 1. Kyle likes to play on the slide.
   2. Lizzie likes to kick a soccer ball.
   3. Viola likes to jump rope.
   4. Tim and his friends like to skate.

Unit 2 Unit Test

I. 1. a, 2. b

(10) 1. Where's the helmet?
      It's between the seesaws.
    2. Where are the swings?
      They're behind the skates.

2. 1. b, 2. c, 3. d, 4. a

3. 1. likes, ride, 2. like, play, 3. likes, kick, 4. like, play

4. 1. 50, 2. 30, 3. 90, 4. 40, 5. 80

5. 1. They like to skate.
   2. They like to play on the seesaw.
   3. He likes to play baseball.

Unit 3 Practice Test

I. 1. b, 2. a, 3. c

(11) 1. Where's the TV?
    2. Where's the dresser?
    3. Where are the stove and the refrigerator?

2. 1. c, 2. b, 3. a

3. 1. cousin's, 2. uncle's, 3. Henry's, 4. aunt's

4. 1. on, 2. next to, 3. It's, 4. in front of, 5. between

Unit 3 Unit Test

I. 1. c, 2. c, 3. b

(12) 1. Where does your mom make dinner?
      She makes dinner in the kitchen.
    2. Where does your family watch TV?
      They watch TV in the living room.
    3. Where does your brother brush his teeth?
      He brushes his teeth in the bathroom.

2. 1. bathroom., 2. living room., 3. kitchen., 4. bedroom.

3. 1. aunt, 2. cousins, 3. brother, 4. uncle

4. 1. table, 2. chair, 3. sofa, 4. DVD player

5. 1. on, 2. in front of, 3. behind

6. 1. It's, 2. They're, 3. It's, 4. They're, 5. They're

Units 1–3 Mastery Test

I. 1. a, 2. b, 3. c

(13) 1. What's she doing?
      She's gluing shapes.
    2. What's he doing?
      He's using the computer.
    3. What's she doing?
      She's coloring a picture.

2. 1. writing, 2. talking, 3. listening, 4. counting, 5. cutting

Answer Key and Audioscript | Level 2

3. 1. are three, 2. is one, 3. are ten, 4. is one

4. 1. 30, 2. 70, 3. 100, 4. 50, 5. 80

   🎧14 1. thirty
       2. seventy
       3. one hundred
       4. fifty
       5. eighty

5. 1. She likes to jump rope.
    2. They like to skate.
    3. He likes to play on the slide.
    4. He likes to ride his bike.
    5. She likes to kick a soccer ball.

6. 1. a, 2. b, 3. a, 4. c

7. 1. It's, 2. It's, 3. They're, 4. They're, 5. It's

8. 1. kick, 2. fly, 3. ride, 4. jump

9. 1. like, 2. likes, 3. like, 4. likes, 5. likes, 6. like

11. 1. a, 2. c, 3. b, 4. a

12. 1. father's, 2. Benjamin's, 3. Gina's, 4. uncle's, 5. Bobby's, 6. aunt's

Unit 4 Practice Test

1. 1. yes, 2. no, 3. yes, 4. yes

2. 1. on, 2. between, 3. next to, 4. on

   🎧15 1. The music store is on Elm Street.
       2. The movie theatre is between the gas station and the train station.
       3. The computer store is next to the café.
       4. The library is on Main Street.

3. 1. a, 2. b, 3. c, 4. b

4. 1. want, 2. wants, 3. want, 4. want, 5. wants

Unit 4 Unit Test

1. 1. T, 2. F, 3. F, 4. T,

   🎧16 1. The supermarket is on the corner of Main Street and River Street.
       2. The café is between the gas station and the bus stop.
       3. The computer store is next to the library.
       4. The train station is on Green Street.

2. 1. It's on Center Street.
    2. No, there isn't.
    3. Yes, there is.
    4. No, there isn't.

3. 1. near, 2. there isn't, 3. want, 4. to buy, 5. There's, 6. between

4. 1. b, 2. c, 3. a, 4. c

5. 1. wants, 2. want, 3. They, 4. Andrew, 5. want, 6. want

Unit 5 Practice Test

1. 1. artist – b, 2. vet – c, 3. chef – a

   🎧17 1. I like to paint pictures. I want to be an artist.
       2. I love animals. I want to be a vet.
       3. I love food. I want to be a chef.

2. 1. teacher, 2. doctor, 3. actor, 4. pilot

3. 1. no, 2. yes, 3. no, 4. yes

4. 1. does, wants; 2. do, want; 3. does, wants; 4. do, want

Unit 5 Unit Test

1. 1. ✓ left photo, 2. ✓ right photo, 3. ✓ left photo

   🎧18 1. What does he want to be?
       He wants to be a doctor.
       2. What does she want to be?
       She wants to be a writer.
       3. What do they want to be?
       They want to be chefs.

2. 1. vet – b, 2. doctor – c, 3. singer – a, 4. teacher – d

3. 1. does, 2. do, 3. do, 4. does, 5. do

4. 1. artist, b; 2. doctor, d; 3. soccer player, c; 4. dancer, a

5. 1. does, 2. wants, 3. do, 4. want, 5. do, 6. want

Level 2 **89**

Answer Key and Audioscript | Level 2

Unit 6 Practice Test

1. 1. does, 2. do, 3. do, 4. does

2. 1. a, 2. b, 3. b, 4. a

3. 1. do, 12 o'clock, 2. does, 7 o'clock,
   3. does, 4 o'clock, 4. do, 9 o'clock

4. 1. She does her homework.
   2. She goes to school on Monday, Tuesday, Wednesday, Thursday, and Friday.
   3. She feeds her cat every day.
   4. Answers will vary.
   🎧19 Hi, I'm Katie. I go to school on Monday, Tuesday, Wednesday, Thursday, and Friday. I only do my homework on Monday and Saturday. I have a cute cat. She's called Molly. I feed her every day.

5. 1. you, 2. I, 3. your brothers, 4. He,
   5. mom, 6. What

Unit 6 Unit Test

1. 1. b, 6:00 or 6 o'clock,
   2. b, 8:00 or 8 o'clock,
   3. a, 12:00 or 12 o'clock,
   4. a, 4:00 or 4 o'clock,
   5. a, 9:00 or 9 o'clock,
   🎧20 He gets up at 6:00.
   School starts at 8:00.
   They eat lunch at 12:00.
   School ends at 4:00.
   He goes to bed at 9:00.

2. 1. get up, 2. eat breakfast, 3. take a shower,
   4. eat lunch, 5. brush teeth, 6. do homework OR
   2, 5, 6, 1, 3, 4

3. Student's own answers

4. Wording may vary slightly:
   1. She goes to bed at 10:00.
   2. She takes a bath at 9:00.
   3. They watch TV at 8:00.
   4. They ride bikes at 5:00. / They ride their bikes at 5:00.

Units 4–6 Mastery Test

1. 1. F, 2. T, 3. T, 4. T
   🎧21 1. The café is on East Street.
   2. The computer store is between the gas station and the post office.
   3. The café is next to the movie theatre.
   4. The movie theater is on the corner of Maple Street and Pine Street.

2. 1. want, 2. to buy, 3. There's, 4. near,
   5. between, 6. There isn't

3. 1. No, there isn't.
   2. Yes, there is.
   3. Yes, there is.
   4. No, there isn't.

4. 1. want, 2. My friend, 3. My brothers,
   4. wants

5. Accept reasonable variations:
   1. The café is on the corner of Pine Street and Center Street. OR The café is next to the movie theater.
   2. They are on Main Street.
   3. The movie theater is on the corner of Maple Street and Pine Street. OR The movie theater is next to the café.

6. 3, 1, 4, 2
   🎧22 1. What do you want to be?
   I like to help people. I want to be a doctor.
   2. What do you want to be?
   I love music. I want to be a dancer.
   3. What do you want to be?
   I want to be a pilot.
   4. What do you want to be?
   I want to be a mail carrier.

7. 1. does, 2. do, 3. do, 4. does, 5. do

8. 1. chef, 2. teacher, 3. actor, 4. artist

Answer Key and Audioscript | Level 2

9. 1. ✗ – 11/eleven o'clock, 2. ✓ – 6/six o'clock,
   3. ✓ – 3/three o'clock, 4. ✗ – 7/seven o'clock
   5. ✗ – 1/one o'clock

   🎧 23 1. What time is it?
   It's one o'clock.
   2. What time are you playing soccer?
   At six o'clock.
   3. What time is the train?
   At three o'clock.
   4. What time is Mary coming?
   At five o'clock.
   5. What time does the movie end?
   Eleven o'clock.

10. 1. at 6:00., 2. a shower in the morning.,
    3. my teeth before bed., 4. school at 8:00.,
    5. lunch at school., 6. their homework at 4:00.

11. 1. e, 2. d, 3. c, 4. a, 5. b

    🎧 24 1. Jason gets up at 6 o'clock on school days.
    2. Mike eats breakfast at nine in the morning.
    3. Karen eats lunch at twelve.
    4. Elaine plays basketball at four.
    5. Sally goes to bed at ten o'clock.

Unit 7 Practice Test

1. 1. b, 2. a, 3. a, 4. b

   🎧 25 1. I like bananas for a snack.
   2. I want spaghetti for dinner.
   3. I like to eat yogurt for lunch.
   4. I help my mom make lemonade.

2. 1. I do, 2. I don't, 3. she doesn't, 4. they do,
   5. he doesn't

4. 1. tomatoes, 2. cheese, 3. potatoes,
   4. carrots, 5. pineapple, 6. chicken

5. 1. She wants mangoes and bananas.
   2. He wants cheese and cookies.
   3. She wants burgers and fries.

Unit 7 Unit Test

1. 1. pineapple, N; 2. tomatoes, Y; 3. spaghetti, Y;
   4. chicken, N; 5. water, N; 6. potatoes, Y

   🎧 26 1. Do you like pineapple?
   No, I don't.
   2. Does he like tomatoes?
   Yes, I think he likes tomatoes.
   3. Do they like spaghetti?
   Yes, they do.
   4. Do you like chicken?
   No, I don't.
   5. Does Andrea like water?
   No, she doesn't.
   6. Does your cousin like potatoes?
   Yes, he does.

2. 1. Do they like corn?
   2. Does she like strawberries?

3. 1. do, 2. Does, 3. does, 4. Do

4. 1. do, 2. potatoes, 3. don't, 4. fruit, 5. apple

5. 1. ✗ 2. ✓, 3. ✓, 4. ✗

Unit 8 Practice Test

1. 1. kangaroo, 2. zebra, 3. hippo, 4. cheetah,
   5. crocodile, 6. monkey

2. 1. No, they can't.
   2. Yes, it can.
   3. Yes, it can.
   4. Yes, they can.

3. 1. climb trees and hang by its tail.
   2. swim. They are strong.
   3. jump. They have pouches.
   4. fly and talk. It has sharp claws.

4. 1. giraffe can't, 2. elephant can't, 3. zebra can,
   4. peacock can, 5. monkey can't, 6. crocodile can;
   4, 2, 1, 3, 6, 5

   🎧 27 1. A giraffe can't climb a tree.
   2. An elephant can't talk.
   3. A zebra can run fast.
   4. A peacock can fly.
   5. A monkey can't fly.
   6. A crocodile can swim.

Level 2

Answer Key and Audioscript | Level 2

Unit 8 Unit Test

1. **1.** hippo – a, **2.** giraffe – b

2. **1.** c **2.** b **3.** a **4.** b

   🎧28 1. It has a long tail, and it can climb.
   2. It can run fast, and it has sharp claws.
   3. It can jump, and it has a pouch.
   4. It has a long trunk and is strong.

3. 1, 3,
   4, 2
   Hi, Linda. What's that?
   Hey, Ben! It's a toucan.
   I like its beak. Can it fly?
   Yes, it can.

4. **1.** No, it can't.
   2. No, they can't.
   3. Yes, it can.
   4. No, they can't.
   5. No, it can't.

Unit 9 Practice Test

1. **1.** c, **2.** b, **3.** a, **4.** c

   🎧29 1. What does Pam do in February?
   She skates on the pond.
   2. What does your family do in August?
   They go on a vacation.
   3. Does Eric play soccer in October?
   Yes, he plays soccer in October.
   4. Do your friends have birthdays in June?
   Yes, they always have a birthday party in June.

2. **1.** September, **2.** December, **3.** May

3. **1.** skate on ice., **2.** it's my birthday!,
   3. in the fall., **4.** the spring.

4. **1.** always, **2.** always, **3.** never

6. **A.** August, **B.** December, **C.** September

Unit 9 Unit Test

1. **1.** a, **2.** b, **3.** a, **4.** a

   🎧30 1. I live in Canada. My favorite month is September. I rake the leaves in September.
   2. I live in Brazil. My favorite month is February. School starts in February.
   3. My favorite month is April. In England there are a lot of flowers.
   4. I'm from the United States. My favorite month is in the summer, in August. I go on vacation with my mom.

2. **1.** always, **2.** never, **3.** always, **4.** always

3. **1.** does, **2.** do, **3.** do, **4.** Do

5. **1.** May, **2.** the, **3.** summer, **4.** always,
   5. month

Units 7–9 Mastery Test

1. **1.** b, **2.** a, **3.** a, **4.** c

   🎧31 1. Do you like spaghetti?
   Yes, I do.
   2. What does mom want from the store?
   She wants a pineapple.
   3. What do you want for lunch?
   Chicken please. I love chicken!
   4. What do you want with the chicken?
   I want potatoes, please.

2. **1.** Do, **2.** does, **3.** do, **4.** does

3. **1.** do, **2.** carrots, **3.** potatoes, **4.** like,
   5. strawberries, **6.** pineapple, **7.** want
   Note: 2, 3 and 5, 6 answers may be reversed.

4. **1.** Yes, she does.
   2. No, he doesn't.
   3. No, she doesn't.
   4. No, they don't.
   5. Yes, they do.

Answer Key and Audioscript | Level 2

5. 1. b, 2. c, 3. b, 4. c

6. 1. T, 2. F, 3. F, 4. T

7. 1. Can, Yes, they can.
2. Can, Yes, it can.
3. Can, No, they can't.
4. Can, Yes, they can.
5. Can, No, it can't.

8. 1. a monkey, 2. an elephant, 3. a kangaroo,
4. a parrot

9. 1. b, 2. b, 3. b

(32) 1. What month is your birthday, Frank?
My birthday's in April.
2. When is the next soccer match?
It's in November.
3. When are you going on vacation?
In August.

10. 1. winter vacation, 2. cousins' visit,
3. birthday, 4. swimming

(33) 1. What does your family do in February?
We go on a winter vacation.
2. What does your family do in August?
My cousins come to visit us.
3. Do you have a birthday in October?
Yes, I do. My birthday is on October 5th.
4. Do you go swimming in July?
Yes, I go swimming in July.

12. 1. always, 2. never, 3. always, 4. never

13. 1. January, 2. skate, 3. don't, 4. winter,
5. favorite

(34) **A:** What do you do in January?
B: I like to skate on the ice. Do you go on vacation in the winter?
A: No, I don't. We never go away in the winter. My favorite month is July.
B: Really? I love July, too.

Level 2 Final Exam

1. 4, 2, 3, 1

(35) 1. They're listening to music.
2. He's gluing shapes.
3. She's writing on the board.
4. They're reading a story.

2. 1. right photo, 2. left photo, 3. right photo,
4. left photo

(36) 1. Do you want an apple or a banana?
A banana, please.
2. Do you want chicken or spaghetti?
I want spaghetti, please.
3. Do you want ham or cheese?
I want some cheese, please.
4. Does Al like lemonade?
Yes, he does!

3. 1. 40, 2. 90, 3. 100, 4. 50, 5. 70

(37) 1. 40
2. 90
3. 100
4. 50
5. 70

4. 1. It's in the bathroom.
2. It's in the living room.
3. It's in the kitchen.
4. It's in the bedroom.

5. 1. T, 2. T, 3. F, 4. T, 5. F

6. 1. d, 2. c, 3. b, 4. a

7. 1. Yes, it can.
2. No, it can't.
3. No, they can't.
4. Yes, they can.

8. 1. ✓, 2. ✗, 3. ✗, 4. ✓

9. 1. She likes to kick a soccer ball OR She likes to play soccer.
2. She likes to jump rope.
3. He likes to play basketball.
4. They like to skate.

10. 1. computer store, 2. post office,
3. restaurant, 4. bookstore

11. 1. What does she want to be?
2. What do you want to be?
3. What does he want to be?
4. What do they want to be?

Level 2 | Notes

Level 2 | Notes

Level 2 | Notes